CHICAGO PUBLIC LIBRARY

Y0-DKL-590

NEW DIRECTIONS FOR TEACHING AND LEARNING

Robert J. Menges, *Northwestern University*
EDITOR-IN-CHIEF

Marilla D. Svinicki, *University of Texas, Austin*
ASSOCIATE EDITOR

Teaching Through Academic Advising: A Faculty Perspective

Alice G. Reinarz
University of Texas at Austin

Eric R. White
Pennsylvania State University

EDITORS

CHICAGO PUBLIC LIBRARY
AUG - 1995
SOCIAL SCIENCES

Number 62, Summer 1995

JOSSEY-BASS PUBLISHERS
San Francisco

TEACHING THROUGH ACADEMIC ADVISING: A FACULTY PERSPECTIVE
Alice G. Reinarz, Eric R. White (eds.)
New Directions for Teaching and Learning, no. 62
Robert J. Menges, Editor-in-Chief
Marilla D. Svinicki, Associate Editor

© 1995 by Jossey-Bass Inc., Publishers. All rights reserved.

No part of this issue may be reproduced in any form—except for a brief
quotation (not to exceed 500 words) in a review or professional work—
without permission in writing from the publishers.

Microfilm copies of issues and articles are available in 16mm and 35mm,
as well as microfiche in 105mm, through University Microfilms Inc., 300
North Zeeb Road, Ann Arbor, Michigan 48106-1346.

LC 85-644763   ISSN 0271-0633   ISBN 0-7879-9955-5

NEW DIRECTIONS FOR TEACHING AND LEARNING is part of The Jossey-Bass
Higher and Adult Education Series and is published quarterly by Jossey-
Bass Inc., Publishers, 350 Sansome Street, San Francisco, California
94104-1342. Second-class postage paid at San Francisco, California, and
at additional mailing offices. POSTMASTER: Send address changes to New
Directions for Teaching and Learning, Jossey-Bass Inc., Publishers, 350
Sansome Street, San Francisco, California 94104-1342.

SUBSCRIPTIONS for 1995 cost $48.00 for individuals and $64.00 for institutions, agencies, and libraries.

EDITORIAL CORRESPONDENCE should be sent to the editor-in-chief, Robert J.
Menges, Northwestern University, Center for the Teaching Professions,
2003 Sheridan Road, Evanston, Illinois 60208-2610.

Cover photograph by Richard Blair/Color & Light © 1990.

Manufactured in the United States of America on Lyons Falls
Pathfinder Tradebook. This paper is acid-free and 100 percent
totally chlorine-free.

CONTENTS

SOCIAL SCIENCES DIVISION
CHICAGO PUBLIC LIBRARY
400 SOUTH STATE STREET
CHICAGO, IL 60605

R01122 69904

1. Educating the Whole Person   5
Robert M. Berdahl

Faculty must know that the major administrators at their institutions value
the activity of academic advising. Demonstration of commitment to effectiveness includes using advising as part of the work load/reward system and
discussing advising with other significant priorities. This forceful "message
from the top" articulates the values held by the leaders and becomes the
expectation of those who are part of the institution.

2. Faculty Speak to Advising   13
James Kelly

Understanding how faculty view academic advising—their role, the institution's commitment, interactions with students—provides a clearer picture
of what happens or does not happen in the name of advising. Compiling and
analyzing these views can lead to organizational change affecting how advising is delivered and by whom. These comments also let faculty know that
they are not alone.

3. Advising Special Populations of Students   25
Diane W. Strommer

Each student is an individual. This chapter draws from the experience of
advisers who address the unique needs of some student groups (honors,
undeclared majors, first-year students, ethnic and cultural minorities, students with disabilities, preprofessional students). The aim is to assist the faculty member who feels underprepared in these situations.

4. Professional Development and Training for Faculty Advisers   35
Carol C. Ryan

The assumption that adviser training is simply the distribution of a catalogue and major checksheets to faculty, along with the exhortation to go out
and advise, needs to be abandoned. Academic advising should not be a hap-
hazard act but rather one emerging from a systematic, continuing training
program, firmly rooted in the faculty culture.

5. Advising in the Arts: Some Thoughts and Observations   43
for Arts Advisers
William J. Kelly

Faculty who advise students pursuing programs in the arts and humanities
often must bring to this endeavor suggestions that should both challenge
the creative spirit of students and reconcile this follow-your-dream attitude
with the realities of earning a living.

12. Resources for Academic Advising 103

Virginia N. Gordon

The literature on academic advising has significantly expanded during the last fifteen years. A clearinghouse, national and regional conferences, and journal articles are available to faculty who want to enhance their knowledge base and develop their skills as academic advisers.

FROM THE SERIES EDITORS

About This Publication. Since 1980, *New Directions for Teaching and Learning* (*NDTL*) has brought a unique blend of theory, research, and practice to leaders in postsecondary education. *NDTL* sourcebooks strive not only for solid substance but also for timeliness, compactness, and accessibility.

The series has four goals: to inform readers about current and future directions in teaching and learning in postsecondary education, to illuminate the context that shapes these new directions, to illustrate these new directions through examples from real settings, and to propose ways in which these new directions can be incorporated into still other settings.

This publication reflects our view that teaching deserves respect as a high form of scholarship. We believe that significant scholarship is conducted not only by researchers who report results of empirical investigations but also by practitioners who share disciplined reflections about teaching. Contributors to *NDTL* approach questions of teaching and learning as seriously as they approach substantive questions in their own disciplines, and they deal not only with pedagogical issues but also with the intellectual and social context in which these issues arise. Authors deal on the one hand with theory and research and on the other with practice, and they translate from research and theory to practice and back again.

About This Volume. In the present issue, Alice Reinarz and Eric White explore how the nature of academic advising has changed over the years and the impact that those changes have on individual faculty. The chapter authors discuss how important the role of faculty is in helping students make their way through the tangled web of decisions they encounter throughout their college years, and how that role eases them into their professional life after college. It is clear that faculty are being called on to play a bigger part in the life of the students. This issue outlines what that part might be.

Robert J. Menges, *Editor-in-Chief*
Marilla D. Svinicki, *Associate Editor*

ROBERT J. MENGES, *editor-in-chief, is professor of education and social policy at Northwestern University, and senior researcher, National Center on Post-secondary Teaching, Learning, and Assessment.*

MARILLA D. SVINICKI, *associate editor, is director of the Center for Teaching Effectiveness, University of Texas at Austin.*

EDITORS' NOTES

Academic advising is an essential element of higher education. Yet few activities have been the subject of such superlative rhetoric and at the same time been reduced to the lowest levels of paper shuffling and bureaucracy. Faculty, especially, have found they are asked, in the name of advising, to be no more than signatories for the many bureaucratic forms that proliferate an advising system.

What has been lost, and that needs recapturing, is the premise that academic advising is teaching. To enable faculty to advise with renewed purpose and dedication, the role of faculty advising must be examined from a teaching perspective. Faculty have long held the mandate to advise. To an extent, they have abdicated this role because of competing demands and expectations. The abandonment of this responsibility has left students without the opportunities to engage faculty in a constructive dialogue about the meaning of higher education in their lives. While faculty have lamented both this loss to students and the absence of this relationship in their lives, little has been done to help faculty renew this role that had once been so vital and that gave such richness to the student–faculty relationship outside the classroom.

Advising has been characterized as a never-ending struggle to "stay current," while laboring with the fear that what is current one day will become misinformation the next. Tools of advising—catalogues, handbooks, manuals, checksheets, and electronic degree audits—abound; and the attention to providing the faculty adviser with the most updated information via high-speed electronics, printed newsletters, or in-person workshops has been laudable.

The expectation that faculty do the advising remains a strong imperative. The perspective, though, that advising is teaching has been lost in the evolution of modern technologies designed to make the more mundane aspects of the job less cumbersome. Consequently, the tools of advising have overshadowed the very raison d'être of the practice. Although the new technologies may have removed some of the more routine aspects from the adviser's repertoire, faculty still are often at a loss, once the checksheet questions have been answered (if they can be answered at all), to have a meaningful dialogue with a student in an advising session. What does the student want to know? What does the student need to know? What should an adviser provide to a student once the degree audit has been run? This volume is designed to enable faculty to understand what it means to be an academic adviser, to see this labor as part of their teaching responsibilities, and to appreciate what faculty are able to contribute to a student's education within the context of the advising interview.

Chapter One provides an administrator's perspective to academic advising. How an institution articulates the need for advising and how this activity is rewarded are often the measures of a successful advising program. As Berdahl notes in his chapter: "Advising, rather than an extension of the educator's role, is integral to it. It is that part of teaching which stretches beyond instruction, beyond lectures and seminars, and reaches students during moments of reflection when they are pondering the future and their place in it." Herein lies the theme of this volume.

Chapter Two analyzes the words of faculty as they view their advising role. Appreciating the advising process from a faculty perspective can be achieved by such an examination. From these words can come greater insights into how advising is perceived and conducted. For those examining an advising program, new approaches to advising may also be suggested.

The institutions of higher education in the late twentieth century comprise a heterogeneous population of students. These students, encompassing such groups as honors, undeclared, and cultural minorities, as well as all other students, should be recognized for the unique characteristics and qualities they bring to our campuses. Chapter Three addresses what faculty should be considering as they are confronted with this diversity of students.

Chapter Four discusses the need not only to train academic advisers, but also to alert faculty to their own need for continuing education and development as advisers.

Chapters Five, Six, and Seven, written by faculty, approach advising from the perspective of the disciplines. It is in the advising context that the history and values of a discipline can be explained to a potential new generation of scholars.

Chapter Eight explores the critical issue of advising women who plan to enter fields in which they have been traditionally underrepresented. As the workforce and college student populations change, care must be taken that when women explore fields that have been difficult to enter in the past, the advising process must facilitate their progress.

Mentoring, while often associated with advising graduate students, is now part of the undergraduate advising vocabulary. This vital aspect of advising undergraduates, so often neglected, needs greater recognition. Chapter Nine provides a basis for this activity.

In Chapter Ten, assessment of advising is explained and encouraged. Via this process, the advising activity can be analyzed and improvements suggested.

Chapter Eleven examines the characteristics of effective teaching and advising, and by noting the similarities between the two areas, supports the thesis that advisers are teachers. The chapter suggests that the dialogue about what constitutes a profession can be addressed to teachers and advisers.

Many faculty are interested in the resources available to comprehend the field of academic advising. These resources are outlined in Chapter Twelve. Conceptual work and research, along with extensive bibliographies, exist. The development of a body of literature for advising provides the insight to approach academic advising with renewed vigor and optimism.

In aggregate, these chapters provide faculty with some of the details of the advising endeavor. Within this context, there are many opportunities to influence the lives of our advisees. Students appear eager to have satisfying advising relationships. While other forums describe the responsibilities of students as advisees, it is our hope that this volume will enable faculty advisers to maintain their part in the advising relationship, not just because somebody needs to do it, but because we can no longer afford to undervalue the significance of this relationship. We owe our students competent and, hopefully, enthusiastic advising.

Academic advising, as practiced by faculty, contributes to the fullness of these students' collegiate years. While faculty naturally appreciate what they provide to students from the classroom podium, the opportunity to extend this teaching to the advising setting represents a significant challenge for those who can value the rewards of being an effective academic adviser.

This volume is written by faculty for faculty. All chapter authors have spent time in the college classroom and have been academic advisers as well. Not all faculty get the opportunity to advise in their disciplines, however. Some are assigned to the exploratory (or undeclared) student, while others may be asked, by virtue of student enrollments, to advise outside of their disciplines. This volume is also intended for faculty who find themselves in these situations.

Ultimately, each advising contract is unique, and each student advised has a special history. The better prepared that faculty are to advise, the more satisfying the contact will be. To that end, this volume is dedicated.

Alice G. Reinarz
Eric R. White
Editors

ALICE G. REINARZ is director of the Undergraduate Advising Center and a senior lecturer in the Department of Microbiology, University of Texas at Austin. In 1990, she received the Carski Foundation Teaching Excellence Award, which is administered by the American Society for Microbiology. The Undergraduate Advising Center has been chosen to receive an Outstanding Institutional Program Award from the National Academic Advising Association for 1995.

ERIC R. WHITE is director of the Division of Undergraduate Studies and affiliate assistant professor of education at The Pennsylvania State University. He has been president of the Association of Deans and Directors of University Colleges and Undergraduate Divisions. He has held elected and appointed positions in the National Academic Advising Association and is currently chair for the Committee on Standards and Ethics in Academic Advising.

In this chapter, the president of a major research university offers his thoughts on academic advising from an administrator's perspective.

Educating the Whole Person

Robert M. Berdahl

> Teaching is an instinctual art, mindful of potential, craving of realizations, a pausing, seamless process, where one rehearses constantly while acting, sits as a spectator at a play one directs, engages every part in order to keep the choices open and the shape alive for the student, so that the student may enter in, and begin to do what the teacher has done—make choices.
>
> —A. Bartlett Giamatti (1988)

It seems almost axiomatic that institutions are impersonal, and large ones even more so. It is their nature, if not their function, to sort people out for the purposes of the institution. The government sorts us one way to collect taxes, the insurance company sorts us another way to collect premiums, and so on. Institutions routinely overlook the unique features of our individuality in order to do business or to serve our needs; they treat us as numbers, albeit with human faces. We are categorized, classified, and ranked regularly in modern life.

Institutions of higher learning are not different, although their ultimate purpose is the opposite of the impersonal. Their purpose is to develop human potential, to give a person's individuality and originality room to produce, and, among other things, to heighten students' knowledge of themselves and others. The goals of colleges and universities are to expand self-realization and to give breath to intellect and personality. One worries, however, that by the time students finish filling out the typical barrage of registration forms, running bureaucratic gauntlets, and working out their class schedules each semester (especially at large universities), their humanity is not exactly liberated as much as it is reduced by the droll rituals of student life. To call the process of higher education dehumanizing goes too far, yet too many students

NEW DIRECTIONS FOR TEACHING AND LEARNING, no. 62, Summer 1995 © Jossey-Bass Publishers

feel lost or alienated. Most students are able to cope, though they are frustrated by the bureaucratic and impersonal aspects of our institutions.

A central question I face as an administrator is—how can we humanize and personalize the undergraduate experience? Small liberal arts colleges obviously have less difficulty with this situation than a large flagship public university with enrollment in the tens of thousands. And large, complex universities should concede, not apologetically, that we simply offer a different kind of experience. Still, I firmly believe that large universities should be able to offer most students a type of a unique relationship, recognizing each student as an individual, and tailoring an education to the person as much as possible. We must also recognize that education takes places both in and outside classrooms and laboratories, and that universities are places in which, ideally, a holistic learning environment exists. Large institutions may have an edge in their ability to offer more diverse learning opportunities. But by far the easiest and most logical point at which a student's relationship with an institution may grow to encompass particular needs, interests, and circumstances lies at the heart of the educational process, in a dialogue between student and teacher. It is in the act and art of teaching, I believe, that we have the best opportunity to respond to students as unique individuals. We have the ability to draw them into relationships with ideas and knowledge in which they may ultimately take responsibility for their own learning, choosing those paths that suit them best. This cannot occur, however, unless teaching is defined expansively to include and embrace the work involved in academic advising.

At large institutions, size and complexity coalesce against the ideal of mentorship. Typically, there are not enough faculty members to go around; the luxury of tutoring and mentoring is not economical. But we have also seen the largely unconfined growth of a culture in academia in which advising plays only a small role in faculty priorities and responsibilities when compared to research, publication, or even classroom performance. In a national survey of faculty conducted in 1989 for the Carnegie Foundation for the Advancement of Teaching and cited by Ernest L. Boyer in his work, *Scholarship Reconsidered,* 71 percent of the respondents from four-year institutions indicated that academic advisement was "fairly unimportant" or "very unimportant" for tenure considerations in their departments. A meager 5 percent said advisement was "very important." As the reward structure offers little in return for time spent advising students, it seems only natural that faculty attention in that area has waned.

Russell Edgerton, president of the American Association for Higher Education, writing in *Change* (1993), said, "In complex universities, students are having trouble getting straight information on things as basic as the courses they need to have for graduation." His commentary on faculty priorities mentions a nascent but potentially promising trend focusing on greater recognition of academic advising as a distinct function for review. A related concern has to do with those who do the advising. New and younger faculty, many of whom may be least knowledgeable of the information one must have in order to render advice effectively in a complex institution, are often those to whom fall the heaviest advising loads. As an alternative to asking inexperienced young faculty members to advise students, universities often have a professional advising staff. Another approach, seldom used, would be to ask senior faculty members—those likely to be most familiar with departmental and institutional requirements and resources—to become more involved in academic advising of first- and second-year undergraduates.

Whether the advising role is taken up by senior or junior faculty, or augmented by professional staff, it should be anchored in the institution's educational mission rather than layered on as a service. Advising, rather than an extension of the educator's role, is integral to it. It is that part of teaching which stretches beyond instruction, beyond lectures and seminars. Its words reach students during moments of reflection when they are pondering the future and their place in it. Done well, it may require a bit of career planning, crisis counseling, and surrogate parenting all rolled into one.

Colleges and universities are more than classrooms. They are communities in which life and learning conjoin. Not every teacher *can*, but the sum of our teaching *must*, address the whole person if the classical idea of educating the whole person, of nurturing physical, spiritual, and intellectual development, is to be kept alive by the university. Teaching and advising need to be part of a seamless process, sharing the same intellectual sphere, informed by a relatively consistent educational philosophy. "In a complex university," wrote Harry Hunt Ransom (1990), "communication is no longer a two-way street. It is a twelve-lane freeway on which variegated 'models,' various speeds, and a thousand varieties of destinations make unity at any one milepost a statistical delusion. But the vision of unity, the human unity, still obtains. A university which loses that vision loses its only significant purpose." The emergence of academic advising as a separate function is a relatively new phenomenon in the history of pedagogy, no doubt aided by the rise of large institutions, complex requirements, more transient faculty, and a less intimate educational process. With the passing of old ideas like apprenticeship and mentorship, a new division of labor has entered education.

Some institutions, hoping to place higher value on academic advising, have addressed the subject in their mission or policy statements. For example, the following was recently added to the General Information Catalog of the University of Texas at Austin:

> The University of Texas at Austin views sound academic advising as a significant responsibility in educating students. Academic advisers assist students in developing intellectual potential and exploring educational opportunities and life goals. Many people in the community contribute to the advising process including faculty, staff, students, and professional advisers. Through the relationship established between adviser and student within a friendly, helpful, and professional atmosphere, a student has the opportunity to:

- Learn about educational options, degree requirements, and academic policies and procedures
- Clarify educational objectives
- Plan and pursue programs consistent with abilities, interests, and life goals
- Use all resources of the University to best advantage.

Ultimately, at the University of Texas at Austin, like most places, the student is responsible for seeking adequate academic advice, for knowing and meeting degree requirements, and for enrolling in appropriate courses to ensure orderly and timely progress toward a degree. Frequent contact with advisers helps students stay abreast of current academic information and promotes progress toward educational goals. The institution's role is to support that progress and encourage effective academic advising campus-wide. While the policy is, in part, a symbolic statement of philosophy, it also establishes academic advising as a high priority of the administration and pledges the institution's support for the function.

Many practical benefits accrue to the student and the institution when academic advising is effective and universally available. First, opportunities for study can be presented to new students who are frequently unaware of the range and diversity of college curricula. First-year students, who may have a somewhat limited vision of their options due to inexperience, immaturity, or parochialism, can benefit enormously from advice that introduces them to a full range of academic choices. Students should probably be encouraged to be more exploratory, to test themselves in a variety of disciplines, and to evaluate their interests and talent in new areas more often. Instead of shunting new students quickly into a narrow curriculum, advisers have a critical role to play in opening new doors by explaining the range of a large university's academic offerings. The efforts and talents of faculty are shortchanged if students are not aware of the programs.

Another direct benefit of attentive advising is that the institution can monitor and pace students' progress toward a degree. A large and complicated problem for many universities is the burgeoning number of students who spend five or more years to complete a bachelor's degree. The availability of space in the university for incoming students is endangered by too many who stay too long. The reasons for taking longer than four years to complete a degree are not always clear, and institutions have begun studying the underlying problems. It is assumed that some delays in progress are beyond the control of the institution (i.e., work and family commitments) and that others will involve considerable discussion among faculty and administrators (reconstruction of curricula, for example). Initially, however, it seems safe to say that more effective advising could help students avoid academic pitfalls and instill more certainty and confidence in them as they engage in the process by which they choose, and stay with, a major.

The adviser should attempt to understand the personal requirements of the student and help tailor a schedule to suit each personal situation, instead of forcing students into a prescribed set of "first-year" courses that may be unsuitable and that result inevitably in wasted time and effort. While I advocate exploration on the part of students, too many false starts and unsuccessful completions add up to frustration for the student and a cumulatively significant inefficiency for the institution. If the level of frustration experienced by a student in an inappropriate academic situation is allowed to build, without some opportunity for the student to reflect on that experience, or without a role model with whom failure can be discussed, the excitement of an undergraduate education will surely be lost.

At different stages in their academic progress, students will require different types of advising. Freshmen are more likely to be worried about their choice of major, are usually uninformed about how to manage their telephone registration process, and may be easily disillusioned if they encounter an academic or personal crisis. Upper-division students may continue to face similar problems, but more often they are concerned about increasing the specialization of their degree plans, looking for graduate or professional school opportunities, or planning for career choices.

It is necessary, therefore, for the academic advising structure to be flexible. The pool of advisers ought to have varied expertise and experience to accommodate transitions in student needs. Additionally, advisers may be a source of key information and connections for linking students to off-campus opportunities. Student volunteerism is one way in which universities provide vital public service in their communities, and advisers are frequently aware of community agencies, programs, and projects that may offer invaluable lessons and experience to undergraduate student volunteers.

Effective advising on a campus-wide basis may well enhance the quality of classes in the long term. Veteran teachers generally agree that some of their most effective work with students is done outside the classroom, and it can reflect positively on the situation faculty members encounter in their classes. By helping guide students into appropriate courses as a part of teaching, the academic adviser ultimately encourages better student-course matches that make for fewer failures, less frustration, and more satisfied faculty. Avoiding the temptation to brush off undergraduates who are seeking advice, faculty who know the rules and resources of the institution, and take the trouble to be helpful, will in the end be helping themselves.

Nurturing scholarly interest and excitement are only part of the academic adviser's role. Advisers are also key figures on campus to help minimize the bureaucratic hassles that some students—and parents—have come to associate with navigating through the channels of the university environment. Specifically, if students learn at freshman orientation that the adviser's information and knowledge of the campus are beneficial, they are likely to return with other questions and concerns. The role of the adviser is crucial to ensuring that students have confidence in the institution, that the institution is perceived as a warm, friendly, and supportive community, and that they aren't being given the run-around. A phone call to expedite a referral to some other office or person can eliminate the campus odyssey of students who, with increasing frustration and fatigue, are sent office-to-office in search of help. Nothing could be more important than for advisers to provide correct, useful and timely assistance, and to go the extra distance by using their knowledge of the institution and its resources and people appropriately and fully.

The advising relationship is crucial to personalizing the undergraduate experience. Students completing a bachelor's degree often report that their initial apprehension upon entering the new world of a university was reduced considerably by the person or persons who helped them get started. While the value of that first personal contact is difficult to quantify, its significance is undeniable. It can be achieved in a variety of ways. At the University of Texas, we have a two-year old program dubbed the "Mooov In," in which administrators, faculty and staff volunteer to help students move into the campus residence halls at the beginning of the fall semester. Whatever initial skepticism there may have been about whether faculty would turn out for the day has quickly been replaced by widespread enthusiasm and participation. The effort has received considerable attention from the press and public and involves hundreds of faculty and staff in a unifying and community-building kind of experience, not unlike an old-time barn-raising. Though it is a small symbolic gesture, parents and students are delighted by what it signifies about the university community. On a campus with too few faculty and staff for the number of students we have, a situation fairly common in public universities, our interactions with students and families are vital to establishing goodwill and public support.

In conclusion, the words of John Stuart Mill, from his writings about liberty and individuality (1961), seem appropriate. "He who lets the world, or his own portion of it, choose his plan of life for him," he said, "has no need of any other faculty than the ape-like one of imitation. He who chooses his plan for himself, employs all his faculties." It ought to be the goal of all advice and counsel we can render to our students, to enable them ultimately to plan for themselves, employing all their faculties, which we must also, and at the same time, help them develop. As Giamatti said, the art of teaching is like sitting as a spectator at a play one directs. Finally Mill goes on to say, "Human nature is not a machine to be built after a model, and set to do exactly the work prescribed for it, but a tree, which requires to grow and develop itself on all sides, according to the tendency of the inward forces which make it a living thing." As we define our greatest responsibilities to younger generations, it seems imperative to me that we ensure that people are the masters and not the tools of institutions, that we seek not to build machines after models or raise generations of imitative apes, but instead give fertile ground to grow mighty trees of human individuality.

References

Boyer, E. L. *Scholarship Reconsidered: Priorities of the Professoriate.* Princeton, N.J.: Carnegie Foundation for the Advancement of Teaching, 1990.

Edgerton, R. "The Reexamination of Faculty Priorities." *Change,* 1993, 25 (4), 10–26.

Giamatti, A. B. *A Free and Ordered Space: The Real World of the University.* New York: Norton, 1988.

Mill, J. S. "On Liberty." In M. Cohen (ed.), *The Philosophy of John Stuart Mill: Ethical, Political and Religious.* New York: Random House, 1961.

Ransom, H. H. *Chronicles of Opinion: On Higher Education: 1955–1975.* Austin: University of Texas Press, 1990.

ROBERT M. BERDAHL is a historian and president of the University of Texas at Austin, where he also holds the Regents Chair in Higher Education Leadership.

The role of faculty in advising has emerged as a point of concern for many colleges and universities. Through surveys, interviews, and videotape presentations, the author has collected faculty attitudes about advising since 1982.

Faculty Speak to Advising

James Kelly

When the great expansion of program offerings, student populations, faculty positions, and physical facilities began in our colleges and universities in the 1950s, little thought was given to how this sudden growth and complexity would affect advising. Advising until that time was characterized by occasional meetings between faculty and students to discuss performance in classes; course planning for the next semester; discussions about recent lectures, classes, or assignments; and at times, talks about personal problems that affected class attendance or deadlines. Little or no preparation was required for these meetings; if paperwork emerged from the advising session, it was typically during a registration period when students needed a faculty signature to enter the registration arena to register for classes.

Advising rosters were small—as few as fifteen or as many as thirty students per faculty member. This number was usually determined by a simple formula: divide the total number of students by the total number of faculty; the result was an individual faculty member's advising responsibility. However, then as now, advising rosters were not a true measure of the advising workload, for roster-based advising completely overlooked in-class students who very likely demanded much more generic advising and discussion time than assigned advisees. The method also ignored drop-in advising for students who walked through the door looking for someone—anyone—to talk to. But the world of higher education was slower and less complex then, and faculty seemed able to find time to meet all of the advising demands of students, as well as to help them in other ways.

NEW DIRECTIONS FOR TEACHING AND LEARNING, no. 62, Summer 1995 © Jossey-Bass Publishers

The Adviser as Helper, Educator, and Mentor

Establishing an early, close connection between faculty and students was often a priority for an institution as well as for individual faculty. One horticulture professor's memory of advising in the 1950s suggests that the process was not only academic:

> Each year when the new freshmen were scheduled to arrive on campus, we would go down to the train station to wait for them. We would help them with their luggage and take them to their living quarters, if necessary. I think that helping like this is part of advising, and I believe that even today faculty could find ways to help. I don't mean going to the train station; that's impossible, because the trains don't run through here anymore (Higginson).

A women's physical education department took a family approach to advising by assigning fifteen new students to instructors who then functioned not only as academic advisers, but who also hosted dinners, planned picnics, organized social events, and acted as an adult friend to their students, from arrival day to graduation (Higginson).

Although advising has become more complex since the 1950s, the concept of adviser as helper remains for some faculty the central role of the adviser:

> As an undergraduate I saw my adviser for 10 glorious minutes each quarter, during which time we discussed Beethoven and mountain climbing (neither of which was my major, need I add?). I see the role of adviser as that of helper, not planner or enforcer. Thus the amount of time I spend with advisees varies from zero to interminable, depending on the student. This is as it should be. Thus, I do not see the need for an adviser's signature on any student forms, from pre-registration to drop-add, etc. All of that detracts from time constructively spent in *advising,* helping (Higginson).

Some advisers believe their role is to educate and broaden the horizons of their students:

> Discussion about scholarly activity is most important. Students need this more than anything else. Stimulation must be provided, interests explored, opportunities on this campus must be explained, interests should be expanded. Examples by professors set. The excitement of "knowing" in many areas should be conveyed to try to do this often. Sometimes I succeed, but not enough. Students' background, narrowness, etc., are hard to overcome. In my opinion they must taste of art, music, literature, science and philosophy, otherwise "I don't consider" them educated (Higginson).

For other faculty, it is critical to infuse moral values into the advising relationship:

I believe the greatest need is for more interaction of faculty and students on a non-academic level, and a greater input of moral values into students' college experience. As far as I can tell, the dorms and student apartments are almost totally student-populated, so the students are exposed only to other students' values. A large amount of drinking, drugs and destructive behavior is evident, and there is a considerable peer pressure in a negative direction, with very little to counter it (Higginson).

The Red Tape View

If helping has characterized one of the positive aspects of advising over time, faculty perceive the downside of advising to be the regulations, red tape, and bureaucracy that have proliferated in our colleges and universities since the 1950s. Using terms that range from resigned to vitriolic, five faculty members were not reluctant to express their dissatisfaction with "red-tape" advising:

The giving and signing of forms should be done by clerks—not faculty. It is not part of academic advising (Higginson).

I would prefer not working as adviser; the clerical procedures could be done more efficiently by an advising unit with expert personnel. I'm bored stiff of signing schedules and drop/add forms. Advising by faculty should be restricted to *academic concerns*, i.e., teaching, research, independent study, and career plans. We should not be bothered with the procedural monkey-business (Higginson).

Once, many years ago at another university I took on the adviser function for about 200 students whose regular adviser was on sick leave. I prepared flow charts of program options and posted them in the hall outside my office. As I recall the average time needed to work with a student was 58 seconds. That experience convinced me that most of advising is a clerk function. The mature student rarely needs "advising." The troubled student has ready access to indexes to social service agencies (Higginson).

Cut out the large number of registration activities. Get rid of such things as early registration, late registration, early drop, Pass-Fail, or if not get rid of these things, at least schedule them to occur at the same time. Let there be a well-defined period during the term where 95% of advising activities can be completed (Higginson).

I am weakest and least interested in giving advice on general degree requirements. How can I help a student choose between Astronomy and BiSci? Someone else should do this. Much of my time is devoted to helping students find their way through the frustrating and unnecessary maze of red tape at this university, getting information that snotty secretaries and pompous professors will not provide. No remedy for this, I guess (Higginson).

Advisers Need Tool Kits, Too

To make matters worse for advisers, not only has there been an increase in rules, regulations, and paperwork, but the post-World War II information explosion has had the same impact on advising that it has had on the way that we live the rest of our daily lives. The mathematics professor who said, "Anybody can advise. What's so difficult about advising? Just give me a catalog and I can advise any student" (Higginson), is certainly unaware of both the quantity and the complexity of the information required for advising. Not since the 1950s—the beginning of the information age—has it been true that "anybody can advise" or that a college catalog is the only resource needed by advisers.

A tool-kit approach to advising indicates the true complexity of the process. The resources or tools in an adviser's kit can number as few as 400 for a small school that admits 120 freshmen. The amount can total 1,000 or more for universities that admit thousands of freshmen. These resources include handouts, checksheets, curriculum guides, program descriptions, course descriptions, class schedules, brochures, handbooks (campus, college, and department), academic calendars, bulletins, memos, computer codes, academic policies, rules, and procedures, in addition to the old, reliable (?) catalog so valued by the mathematics professor.

Although large, this list is far from comprehensive. Flesh it out by calculating the number of curriculum guides (10?, 200?), course descriptions (100?, 4,000?), handbooks (1?, 100?), computer codes (200?), and miscellaneous academic information pieces (50?, 300?) that would be required to advise any students who might walk through a faculty member's door. Certainly the advising tool kit for any institution, large or small, contains more than a college catalog (Kelly, 1988).

Administrators Need an Advising Education

Unfortunately, academic administrators are often unaware of the sheer weight of information that advisers must now handle, and they underestimate or ignore the complexity that characterizes advising today. One urban campus administrator who has great expectations of his faculty, but who very likely has no understanding of his institution's advising tool kit, proposes the following: "Faculty members must reassume responsibility for academic advising, instead of turning it over to non-faculty personnel" (Lazerson and Wagener, 1992). This solution is clearly a reaction to the unparalleled expansion that higher education has experienced since the 1950s. He continues:

> Academic and other services to students have grown exponentially over the last two decades. . . . Simultaneously, academic advising on many campuses has shifted from faculty members to professional staffs. Older students and academically less-prepared students have required substantial tutoring and counseling. To meet their needs, many administrators have set up advising offices and

tutoring centers. Because faculty identity and ego are derived from teaching and research, not from advising students, faculty members have put up little resistance. As a result, institutions are paying extra staffs for academic services (Lazerson and Wagener, 1992).

It is certainly true that a shift has occurred at many institutions; a cadre of advising professionals or specialists has emerged at both large and small schools, where, until this period in history, advising by anyone other than a faculty adviser was strictly prohibited. However, the emergence of professional or full-time advisers is not the product of institutions admitting older students or less well-prepared students. It is the result of increased student populations that may require advising rosters of 100–600 students (not 15–30); curricular complexity; a continuous flow of information (both academic and nonacademic, delivered in print or electronically, or both) to advisers; and greater demands on faculty to increase class sizes, teach more courses or sections, publish, conduct research, serve on committees, and provide public service. Add to this the contents of an institution's advising tool kit and it becomes apparent that a return to faculty-only advising is not just unrealistic, but it would also prove to be overwhelming, perhaps impossible, at many institutions. Nevertheless, the urban campus administrator's solution continues:

> We can think of some specific measures that would strengthen advising and cut costs. Faculty members could be asked to reassume the responsibility for freshman advising, doing away with special offices set up for that purpose. Undergraduates at large institutions often have no contact with faculty members outside classes during their first year, and this is detrimental to their education. . . . Faculty members could advise about courses and career paths, and, if they lack the information, they should learn it. The arguments that "faculty lack the knowledge" or that "it is a misuse of their expertise" are too much like the "women are more suited for housework than men" argument to suit us. That faculties now do not do advising well is not a sufficient excuse to let the current situation continue (Lazerson and Wagener, 1992).

For many faculty, it is not a question of not advising well; it is the recognition that advising today is far different from what it was twenty, thirty, or forty years ago. Furthermore, this difference is not the result of the influx of older students or of students who are not as well prepared academically.

Student Characteristics: Critical Factor #1. As today's students progress from high school to college, they express a high degree of uncertainty about their eventual choice of major. Many students overestimate their ability to earn good grades and underestimate the number of study hours required to earn these grades. Except for those who intend to study agriculture or physical education, they know little about the majors that they are considering. Many students expect to change majors at least once in their college careers. Hence, the challenges that students bring to advising sessions include the following:

academic uncertainty, unrealistic attitudes about the demands of college and the expectations of faculty, little knowledge or experience related to their intended program of study, and a predisposition to change (Kelly, 1993). The advising role has become far more complex and time-consuming than advising "about courses and career paths." And even those two responsibilities are significantly more difficult than they were in the past. When administrators or senior faculty view advising as a simple affair of course scheduling or form signing, it is a sure sign that they have not carried a full advising roster of freshmen or sophomores for some years.

Availability: Critical Factor #2. For many faculty, paramount concerns are to find time for advising and being available at a specific location:

> Availability is probably the hardest job for most faculty. The best opportunities for advising often occur in the classroom. I would guess that some of my best advising is the offhand things I say in class (Kelly, 1988).

> My philosophy of advising: be there, be available. I try to keep about 6 hours a week for advising; I don't know if that is a good amount or not. I try to have a group meeting time at least once a week. It's a time when students just walk in and we talk (Kelly, 1988).

> I give my home phone number to every student that I advise and to every student in my classes. I do that, but I'm not saying every faculty member should (Kelly, 1988).

Some faculty adhere to the letter of the law and are available in their offices, but keep hours that are few and far between or that are generally not compatible with most students' schedules. These are the advisers who post hours such as Monday and Thursday 7:30 to 8:30 A.M., or M-W-F 11:30 A.M. to 12:30 P.M. The earlier hours conflict with breakfast time, eight o'clock classes and rush hour; the mid-day times interrupt class hours and lunch time. It is most effective to hold office times on the same days and hours each week. It is also advisable to start appointments at the half-hour.

Some advisers respond to the availability issue by maintaining office hours by appointment, but that is hardly a solution for students who cannot predict when they will need to contact their adviser.

> One thing that bewilders me is when my colleagues post a sign on their doors: office hours by appointment. Well, if I want to call or talk to one of these about a student, or to ask for information, how can I make an appointment if they are not available in their offices (Kelly,1988)?

Rewards: Critical Factor #3. Advisers who are conscientious and committed can become jaded, or, if they are blessed with a sense of humor, may cast advising in a light that is both cynical and whimsical:

On bad days I think of the academic side of the university as housework. If that's true, then advising is like dishwashing. Actually, advising does have a lot of characteristics of dishwashing: it's neglected; it causes a great deal of problems; and, one of the hardest things is, if you get good at it . . . for example, when I was a graduate student living with other students, the worst problem for us was dishwashing, and if somebody was actually sensitive to the problem and washed the dishes, they would end up doing that all the time. Likewise, if you get good at advising, then that's about all you'll be able to do (Kelly, 1988).

Stated in less analogous terms,

Faculty get very few or no rewards for their efforts in this area. If anything, the better advisers get more advisees, and have even less time for the major promotion and tenure categories! Faculty, however, have a "moral" obligation to help students get the most out of their education, and this necessitates good advising and, unfortunately, time stolen from other necessary tasks. Also—advising loads are very uneven across faculty/departments/colleges! (Higginson).

Rewards, of course, can be the sticking point for many faculty when advising is discussed. They often feel that they are on the horns of a dilemma: on the one hand, advising could be considered a moral obligation; on the other, too much time spent in advising can hurt rather than help faculty careers:

If we say that advising is really important, and we see a program thriving—a program that relies essentially on successful advising—and as a result of success there are more students and more time demanded and more lives affected, and no reductions in other expectations or increases in rewards or training to deal with the types of real life problems this person is likely to confront, or any give whatsoever in the system to recognize this, then it doesn't take long for an intelligent person to recognize that there is a whole bunch of pious lipservice about advising, but it really doesn't rank up there very high in the university's priorities. I do think that there is a reason for someone in authority somewhere to say more than thanks, and that's a hellava problem—what do you propose we do, etc. Even altruism has limits for those of us who lack Francis of Assisi's sanctity (Higginson).

All full-time faculty are advisers at my campus. To my knowledge, there is no compensation such as a lighter teaching load or a salary adjustment for this service. Advising does not count when one is reviewed for promotion or tenure. There should be some adjustment for this important service (Higginson).

Though advising is like a religious duty, it does not really pay the average professor to invest too much time in it. It is research and publications that constitute the plasma of promotion and tenure. It is also research and publications, not good teaching or advising, that make a professor marketable. In addition,

> many students do not seem to be interested in good advising. Consequently, we should not push it upon them. Anyway, the administration has us going crazy with teaching, research, committees, and so on. How much can they squeeze? (Higginson)

> Course release time should be given for advising (Higginson).

> Academic advising will never be worth a damn until the university provides *incentives* for advising—e.g., MONEY. Only then will it be worthwhile for faculty to take time away from research—which is what earns promotion and financial rewards (Higginson).

Indeed, *poor advising* is rewarded by relieving faculty of advising loads or decreasing their responsibilities.

Somewhere Between Beethoven and Mickey Mouse

As recurrent as the discussion of rewards, is the debate concerning the importance of advising:

> I think advising is not important. My concern is with the student's chosen major, not with the "Mickey Mouse" activities which go under the heading of "General Education" and accomplish little except keep people in jobs. If you question my advisees, you will learn that I give them all the time they need, and that I bend over backwards to help them. However, advising would be much easier if some of the rules were made more sensible and the high schools really prepared students for a university education (Higginson).

> Academic advising at my campus, for the most part, is a farce since you advise people who are not in your discipline and who do not want to be advised (Higginson).

> I think academic advising is largely a waste of time in our department. Students of college age and ability should be able to choose their own courses and should have the responsibility for doing so on their own. Most advising functions are concerned with treating the student as though he were still in high school. This is demeaning to the student and deprives him of the opportunity to be responsible for his own well-being (Higginson).

For the most part, however, faculty place high value on advising. They believe the adviser to be very influential in the total education of students:

> Advising for the undergraduate level is extremely important. Students need more than a "canned" education. They need time given to assist them in developing into a total person in addition to their educational pursuits. Students need assis-

tance in selecting optional courses, appropriate to their career and alternative courses when substitutions can be made. It's the adviser who can best know the student and positively challenge them (Higginson).

The role of the adviser is probably the most important role, or if it isn't the most important, it is at least as important as an above-average teacher. In other words, I put it rather high on the list of priorities (Kelley, 1988, 89).

Very important, especially first two years (Higginson).

Advising is important and should be taken seriously by advisers. I think the system is less in need of reform than individual faculty are in need of a stronger sense of responsibility to advisees. But I don't know how to *enforce* that—people tend to have it or not (Higginson).

Whether or not faculty believe that advising is important, it is incumbent upon colleges and universities to provide advising for their students and to determine who (faculty, professionals, graduate students, undergraduates, or a combination of one or more of these) will provide the service. In addition, central administration, deans, and department chairs must encourage advisers to learn or at least to recognize the contents of their institution's advising tool kit. Ideally, the institutions should provide opportunities for training.

When asked for suggestions to improve advising on their campuses, faculty often express a sincere desire for training sessions or advising workshops:

The hardest thing for a new faculty member to do is to get started in advising. New faculty need advising seminars or anything that would help them in advising (Higginson).

I would like to suggest a basic programmed text on advising for new faculty. A format similar to Mager's paperback on behavioral objectives would be excellent. I am concerned that in my advising I am missing things I shouldn't because I know so little, and there's much to be aware of in our complex system. People have been most helpful, but I have to ask and keep asking because much information, especially the most basic, is taken for granted and never stated. For example, I only became aware of the deficiency points by accident, and almost lost a student over the process. I still don't know exactly how the formula works (Higginson).

Each college should provide formal training for new advisers. The technical aspects are extremely confusing to a newcomer. Several training sessions of an hour or two each would greatly aid in the mechanics of advising (Higginson).

All faculty need to be educated and rewarded for this important process. Some ways are through orientation week workshops and singling out exceptional advisers for recognition (Higginson).

Efforts should be made to have in-service training for faculty (novice and veteran alike) as part of an on-going process. And last, but not least, faculty should be recognized and rewarded for exemplary advising. What do you think will happen (Higginson)?

Whose Job Is It Anyway?

Faculty who do not see themselves as advisers are quick to make recommendations about who should or should not assume responsibility for advising:

A lot of the best advising that goes on on campus is what students do for each other (Kelly, 1988).

As a full-time extension professor, I have only a peripheral view of undergraduate advising. However, I have a son who is a freshman. The amount of advice he is getting could well be done by an astute departmental secretary (Higginson).

I believe academic advising is extremely important. Advisers should have twenty or so advisees—enough to make it worthwhile but not burdensome. I don't believe in students and/or secretaries substituting for advisers (Higginson).

Advising does take up a lot of the faculty member's time which he/she could be using to concentrate on research. In many instances the graduate students do advising, not the faculty (Higginson).

Advising is of extreme importance and a senior level student might be of great assistance to incoming/beginning students along with assigned faculty advisers (Higginson).

I believe that student advising and self-advising are scandalous ideas. Somehow, this university should have the manpower and dedication to do a good job advising—possibly by committee with regularly scheduled office hours, if need be. After many years, I believe that the situation is still marginal to poor, as far as most undergrads are concerned (Higginson).

Personally, I enjoy contact with students, but I often feel very uninformed and then uninformative. This is one area of university activity which may well benefit by the division and specialization of labor; that is informed, professional counselors would probably be better for students than are faculty, at present (Higginson).

Consensus? Who Needs It?

We have left the most basic question unanswered. What is advising? We certainly do not lack definitions. The literature is full of them; however, what is lacking is anything resembling a consensus definition. Some would ask, Why do we need a definition? Why should we seek consensus? There are those who identify advising with helping students to make decisions; others view it as an extension of teaching; some see it only in terms of bureaucracy and red tape; others link it to the educational mission of their institution; more than a few consider it nothing more than signing forms; precious few envision it as ten glorious minutes each quarter discussing Beethoven and mountain climbing.

We all know advisers who are as definite and outcomes-oriented about advising as St. Benedict was in the sixth century when he specified the procedure for receiving brothers into the Church:

> A senior chosen for his skill in winning souls should be appointed to look after them with careful attention. The concern must be whether the novice truly seeks God and whether he shows eagerness for the Work of God, for obedience and for trials. The novice should be clearly told all the hardships and difficulties that will lead him to God (Fry, 1982).

We also recognize the adviser-type who helps students through the maze of academic choices:

> A good adviser has to help students sort. One example of sorting is to help students sort this incredible array of requirements that we have come up with (Kelly, 1988).

Then there is the adviser whose primary mission is to impart a sense of reality to his or her advisees:

> I deal mostly with honors students, and every honors student has a grandmother like Dan Quayle's, who told them that they could do anything that they wanted to. One of my first jobs is to point out all of the things that they can't do (Kelly, 1988).

Finally, there is the type of adviser who is not really sure what advising is or what it should accomplish:

> My philosophy of advising is, follow your bliss. Students need to be more intuitive about their decisions, like the young woman who came to my office one day and told me that she wanted to change her major from physics to English. I'm an English professor, so you can imagine how astonished I was. "Why would you abandon physics in order to study literature and writing," I asked her. "Are you having difficulty with the math or the science required?" "No," she said, "I just like English more than physics." This is a woman who was following her bliss (Kelly).

Joseph Campbell puts it this way:

> Have you ever read Sinclair Lewis's *Babbitt?* Remember the last line? "I have never done the thing that I wanted to in all my life." That is a man who never followed his bliss. I always tell my students, go where your body and soul want to go. When you have the feeling, then stay with it, and don't let anyone throw you off.

> If you do follow your bliss you put yourself on a kind of track that has been there all the while, waiting for you, and the life that you ought to be living is the one you are living. When you can see that, you begin to meet people who are in the field of your bliss, and don't be afraid, and doors will open where you didn't know they were going to be (Campbell, 1988).

Somewhere between the poles of telling "all the hardships and difficulties" and encouraging students to follow their bliss lies that comfortable (or perhaps, uncomfortable) niche that each of us could describe as our own special theory and practice of advising. If it is done well, with good will,

> Advising is not only one of the requirements of our job, it is one of the most rewarding parts of our job (Kelly).

References

Campbell, J., with B. Moyers. *The Power of Myth.* New York: Doubleday, 1988.

Fry, T. (ed.). *The Rule of St. Benedict in English.* Collegeville, Minn.: Liturgical Press, 1982, 78–79.

Higginson, L. C., Kelly, J. J., Wall, H. W., White, E. R., and Wyckoff, J. H. *Academic Advising Analysis.* University Park: The Pennsylvania State University, 1982.

Kelly, J. J. "The Penn State Advising Tool Kit." *NACADA Journal,* 1988, *8* (2), 42–46.

Kelly, J. J. *Faculty Perspectives on Advising.* University Park: Pennsylvania State University, 1988, 1989. (Videotape.)

Kelly, J. J. *Freshman Characteristics Profile, 1992–93.* University Park: Pennsylvania State University, 1993.

Lazerson, M., and Wagener, U. "Rethinking How Colleges Operate." *Chronicle of Higher Education,* Sept. 30, 1992, p. A44.

JAMES KELLY is senior associate director, Division of Undergraduate Studies, at The Pennsylvania State University, University Park.

To be rewarding for both faculty and students, advising special popula-
tions of students requires understanding their needs and identifying
strategies to facilitate their learning.

Advising Special Populations of Students

Diane W. Strommer

Many faculty are likely to remember their first day of advising, if at all, as a blur of faces and a trip into the hitherto unknown and unexplored territory of the institutional catalog and university regulations. Some never move beyond the notion that advising is service as a human catalog and checklist of requirements. Advising so defined does not include the need to understand changing populations of undergraduates—or any special groups within the student body—or to facilitate their learning; it misses both the joys and opportunities advising offers faculty.

Although nationally the "faculty-only model [of advising] has been and continues to be the primary organizational model for advising across all institutions" (Habley, 1993, p. 21), advising is not a responsibility most new faculty actively seek, think about, or for which they prepare. While many institutions require all faculty to advise, any training offered typically is a workshop of less than a day with the content primarily conveying information (Habley, pp. 60–61). The practice of what has been called the "dump and run" method of adviser selection and training continues alive and well in higher education. (Good news! You're the new departmental adviser. Registration is next Tuesday.)

Performing what a catalog or, better yet, a computer can do for a student does not yield much satisfaction for the faculty adviser. To define advising as to give information and to check course schedules is to limit its potential as a rewarding experience for both adviser and student. More broadly conceived, advising encompasses at least five levels of activity:

1. Providing basic information about courses and curricula.
2. Individualizing the academic program.

New Directions for Teaching and Learning, no. 62, Summer 1995 © Jossey-Bass Publishers

3. Assisting the student in identifying educational goals and in achieving them through institutional resources.
4. Fostering students' capacity for lifelong learning by developing advising tasks that teach goal setting, planning, and decision making and that provide practice in gathering and synthesizing information.
5. Creating a loop through which information about a changing student body and students' backgrounds, expectations, and goals may influence classroom practices, student learning, and campus life.

Unfortunately, while many advisers never consider activities that go beyond the first two levels of advising, students identified as members of a "special population" primarily need the advising associated with levels three, four, and five.

We need to reconceive not only what we do in the name of advising, but how we do it as well. As the Task Group that produced *A New Vitality in General Education* noted, too often "we practice advising as a form of telling and feel the compulsion to make authoritative statements beyond our knowledge and experience, rather than concentrating on listening and enabling the students to explore and make their own decisions" (Association of American Colleges, 1988, p. 43). The more institutions implement computerized degree audit and telephone registration systems, the less advising on level one is necessary. Instead, faculty can focus on students and their learning, and on the educational opportunities that afford them the greatest potential for growth and development.

By structuring the advising of a special population of students into small, collaborative groups of five to seven advisees, an adviser can facilitate student learning by designing appropriate tasks and assigning them for cooperative solution. Just how does one make a decision about a major, for example? Assign a group of undecided students the task of finding out. Give them some clues to help along the way, and meet with them frequently to check their progress.

Giving small groups of students who have a need in common a task to work on collaboratively not only engages them, but also helps them to become more effective learners. Advising through collaborative groups is an instructional approach worthy of faculty attention (see, for example, Goodsell, Maher, and Tinto, 1992, and Johnson, Johnson, and Smith, 1991).

Points of Transition in the Undergraduate Years

The research clearly demonstrates that most critical influences on students' persistence and success in college are involvement with a peer group centered on an academic task and out-of-class contact with faculty (Astin, 1993; Pascarella and Terenzini, 1991). While this research supports the need for continuing contact with faculty advisers, students' needs for advising and mentoring relationships do vary as they progress through college. Although students may experience transitional crises at any time, certain points tend to be more stressful than others, and students at these times will benefit from close faculty attention. Virtually all students of all ages and academic conditions, for example, find the transition to college to be challenging and somewhat disruptive to their self-esteem, especially during the first semester. Many first-year students, particularly those who are of the first generation to attend college, enter an academic culture for which little has prepared them. Challenged and bewildered by the options the contemporary college offers, many first-year students are conscious primarily of their own academic inadequacies and of the extraordinary cost of erroneous choices.

As they contemplate the end of the undergraduate years, seniors confront another difficult transition to the next stage—a job or graduate or professional school. Along the way, students have passed through several significant points of transition: confirming a major, changing one, being denied access to the chosen field of study, preparing for and returning from an off-campus experience like study abroad, making connections between academic study and off-campus programs of community service, internships, or clinical work.

Today's Undergraduates

Understanding any special population of students requires noting some changes within today's undergraduates as a whole, diverse as they are. Despite the stories we tell about them, today's students are no less bright than those of any other generation, no more responsible for the culture that produced them, and no more sanguine about what is required to prepare for their futures. Nonetheless, some generalizations do accurately describe college students today:

1. They are inadequately prepared in terms of general knowledge and basic skills. While they may know an astonishing amount about a given topic, they have huge gaps in what faculty often assume "everyone knows." Many do not read with ease or skill, particularly when confronted with difficult texts.
2. While some students have strong quantitative skills and science backgrounds, many are not only poorly prepared, but also are so anxious about their ability to learn in these areas that they avoid any field of study requiring math or science.
3. The range of their experience in dealing with information systems, particularly computing, is extremely wide, with some students more expert than many faculty, and others having no experience at all.
4. While recognizing the necessity of a college degree, many are neither naturally inclined toward academic work nor highly motivated to do it.
5. Often the product of complex family situations, many bring considerable personal and psychological problems with them to college. Appearing to be more highly stressed and prone to depression, students today seek psychological counseling more frequently than ever before.

6. They are more bewildered about how best to prepare appropriately for their futures. The accelerating rate of change in business outlook and employment patterns, among other things, makes it difficult to anticipate which critical skills and areas of knowledge will be advantageous to continued employment.

7. Many work long hours, incur staggering debt, or do both to obtain a college degree. For this reason, among others, students and their parents often behave more like consumers than supplicants and expect a certain value and services for their investment.

Other observers of today's undergraduates have noted the defining events for this generation and their pessimism (Levine, 1993), the dominance of the concrete and experiential in their learning styles (Schroeder, 1993), or their high school experiences that inadequately prepare them to learn effectively (Erickson and Strommer, 1991). All agree that today's students bring new learning needs with them to college.

Advising Special Populations of Students

That which constitutes a special population of students varies from campus to campus, but typically the term refers to any group requiring special attention. Some groups are singled out because their backgrounds make their connection to higher education especially fragile; their journey from entering freshman to graduating senior is more tenuous than that of other students. Others have special talents and skills that we are obligated to nurture and strengthen.

What constitutes effective advising for "special" populations does not differ markedly from effective advising practices for all students. If resources were bountiful, the services and advising practices recommended for special populations would no doubt enhance the educational experiences of all students and would provide a more powerful link between the student and the college.

Advising special populations of students calls for structure and intrusiveness, contact with individuals, or, preferably, small groups of students made routine by weekly, biweekly, or monthly meetings. Encounters should not be left to chance or the demands of registration. Advisers and advisees need to plan the content of these advising sessions and need to develop precise goals and tasks to achieve them to meet the students' needs at particular times in the undergraduate years.

On a given campus, one group of students may be moved to the foreground for special attention for a time and then returned to the background. While once women once were a "nontraditional," special population on many campuses, today they are in the majority. Even so, a group like women majoring in engineering may continue to benefit from special advising and mentoring if they are to succeed in a field dominated by men and in courses in which the climate may continue to be chilly for them (Hall and Sandler, 1982).

Although some of the characteristics of special populations of students and effective advising practices for them are touched on separately below, students themselves do not, of course, slip smoothly into our categories. A student may have both a disability and the qualifications for honors work; she may be both underprepared and undecided about a choice of major; he may be a member of an ethnic minority and a pre-med student. Our concern, as always, should be to use categories to help us to anticipate students' needs and concerns but never to mask the uniqueness of each.

Academically Underprepared Students. The jargon differs. At one college, students whose previous background and grades are deemed lower than the usual standard for admission may be called "developmental," while at another college a similar group might be referred to as "provisionally admitted," under "conditional status," or by a more positive label or acronym.

An adviser would note that the most important characteristic of many underprepared students is their low self-esteem and lack of confidence in themselves as learners. All new students need "validating experiences," reassurance that they can indeed make it in college (Terenzini, 1993, p. 6), but underprepared students need it in double measure. To choose a metaphor from sports, being an enthusiastic coach egging on a winning team conceptualizes the adviser's role with underprepared students.

Some students with poor preparation are academically ambitious and are too impatient to take the time to develop skills essential for continued academic success. Such impatience is characteristic of some recent immigrants who may be very bright but whose academic backgrounds have huge gaps and whose commands of English are shaky.

The adviser's toughest tasks with both groups of underprepared students are to gain an accurate reading of the level of their basic skills, to ensure that students take the essential steps to fill gaps before moving into mainstream courses, and to provide the right mixture of challenge and support. Underprepared students often need the help of supplemental instruction, study tables, or tutoring. They, more than any other students, benefit from learning groups that are built into or that exist along with their academic courses.

The faculty adviser who understands the needs of these students can play a key role with colleagues by helping them to understand the student's distinct requirements as learners. "Dumbing down" courses helps no one; underprepared students need faculty who believe that they can learn, hold high expectations for their performance, carefully monitor their progress, and provide the academic support to enable them to reach their goals.

Students Undecided About a Choice of Major. Recently, after an orientation program for new students, an engineering faculty member came up to me. "What's this business about undeclared majors?" he asked. "Do you really mean that students come to the university not knowing what they're going to major in?" His incredulity might be rare, but the perception that being undecided about one's major is somehow at odds with college-going is not. While we talk a good game about the purpose of college extending far beyond preparation for a career—or a job—most people do expect that the primary purpose of a college education is in fact to prepare for a career, and that the major is the route by which to travel. Even if the facts are that most undergraduate majors do not correlate with a person's eventual career and that people today change careers three or four times, the connection between major and career remains tenacious.

Students who have yet to select a major thus often enter college feeling even more uncertain than other first-year students about their legitimacy as college students. Institutions that do not allow "undecided" or "undeclared" as an admissions category or those that segregate students into separate admissions units can intensify those feelings. Students need assurance that indecision is normal—one third to one half of all entering students are estimated to be undecided to some extent about their choice of major—and they need assistance in determining a sequence of steps to follow to make an appropriate choice.

A brief sorting questionnaire is a very useful first step for determining the extent of students' undecidedness. The questionnaire could ask the following questions:

Check the following statements that most closely correspond with your feeling about your major and career at this time:

1. I know what I want to major in; it is ___.
2. I know what field I wish to work in after graduation. It is ___.
3. I am still deciding between two or more fields of study. They are _____.
4. I know I am interested in the general area(s) of _____.
5. I have no idea what career I want to pursue.
6. I have no idea what major I want to study.
7. Check those fields of study which interest you somewhat from the list below and draw a line through any you would not consider. (Include a list of the majors offered at your institution.)

Going through this exercise provides valuable information for advising. The first question uncovers students who actually have selected a major, a fact that the registration system may not yet have recognized. The remainder of the questions allow you to sort between several very different groups of undecided students. Advisers often observe that undecided students are, in general, a bimodal group. Some are extremely capable students sorting through their many options; others have yet to identify any area of real academic strength.

At the core of selecting a major or career field are self-knowledge and understanding one's talents, skills, and preferences. Many students come to a closer understanding of themselves through conversations in small groups about such matters. Other effective strategies to help students move toward the selection of a major include computerized career guidance programs (such as SIGI Plus or Discover), interviewing department chairs, shadowing a senior or a recent graduate in a prospective major, doing volunteer work in an area of interest, interning, keeping exploration journals, and analyzing courses for the transferable skills they develop. Undecided students are more likely to participate in these activities if they are working collaboratively in a group on structured tasks or in workshops and courses designed to help them assess the relationships between their interests, abilities, and values and those required for a particular career.

Students with Disabilities. The difficult transition from high school to college faced by the majority of new college students is intensified for those with disabilities. Even so, greater numbers of students with disabilities are entering higher education each year. Among the new freshmen in the fall of 1992, 9.6 percent identified themselves as having a disability; 23 percent of these, or 2.2 percent of the entire freshman population, identified themselves as having a learning disability, double the percentage so identified just four years earlier (*Chronicle*, A30, "The American Freshman," 1993).

Sometimes a student's disability is readily apparent; at other times it is not. Some students do not seek accommodation for "hidden" disabilities such as epilepsy, visual impairments, hearing impairments, and learning disabilities because they fear being labeled, do not want to be perceived as different from their peers, or have had negative reactions from faculty or teachers in the past. Some students, particularly those with learning disabilities, experience failure before acknowledging that a disability exists.

Many students have been diagnosed as having a learning disability long before entering college, but some have not. A pattern of uneven abilities—a major disparity, for example, between math and verbal SAT scores, or grades that are totally out of balance with the amount of effort a student is making—warrant a referral for testing.

At most colleges, a person or an office is responsible for interpreting the Americans with Disabilities Act of 1990 and other relevant federal and state legislation for the campus community and for designing a campus accommodation system. Advisers should familiarize themselves with that system so they know which support services to recommend to students and how to advocate for them when necessary.

Despite any limitation they may have, students who have a disability understandably want faculty and peers to focus on their abilities, to reduce any barriers that still exist to their full participation in campus life, and to give them the support and encouragement all students need. Most faculty willingly accommodate the needs of students with visual, hearing, and mobility impairments, but some have a difficult time understanding a similar need to accommodate students with learning disabilities. As Jonathan Cohen notes, "Most universities, and most student affairs professionals, faculty, and mental health professionals, have not yet come to grips with what it means to identify, diagnose, teach, and counsel the learning disabled student" (Cohen, 1984, p. 30). Students with a learning or any other disability, we must realize, do not seek an easier route to a college degree. What they do ask is not to be penalized for a disability they cannot control.

Members of Racial and Ethnic Minorities. No campus is free of racial or ethnic prejudice. Campuses with fewer than 30 percent minority students typically offer the most inhospitable climate for them. Overt and subtle behaviors on the part of faculty, staff, and other students frequently make the minority student feel "marginal, conspicuous, and isolated from the mainstream of the institution" (Green, 1989, p. 114). Advisers, particularly, need to be sensitive to the climate for minority students on their campus and need to understand their special concerns. Training in intercultural communications can be particularly valuable for academic advisers.

By enlisting the aid of peer advisers or working with students in multicultural groups, advisers can create a more welcoming climate for students who are members of racial and ethnic minorities. Special orientation and other programs for students' families to involve them in the life of the campus and to help them understand the opportunities and pressures also strengthen the support network for minority students.

While few faculty are ever intentionally discriminatory in their dealing with students, giving advice on the basis of untested assumptions or making judgments on the basis of culturally derived behavior can have the same effect. Some African-American students are underprepared for college level work; but others are Merit Scholars. Some Latino students come from poor inner-city schools; others from the finest private preparatory schools. Some Asian-American students come from families that have been U.S. citizens for three or more generations; others are recent immigrants. Although Latino, Native American, and African-American students graduate from college at a lower rate than white students, Asian-American students graduate at a higher rate than any other group. The student who does not speak up may not be passive; the student who refuses eye contact may not be shifty. Each may instead be demonstrating the preferred cultural behavior.

This diversity within each racial and ethnic minority group is such, in short, that generalizations are highly suspect. Although it is important for advisers to understand the special pressures of being a minority student on a white campus, what is most important is to build a trusting relationship with the students, to try to determine their needs, and to provide the encouragement and support of all campus resources to involve them in campus life and to help them to attain their goals.

Honors Students. Most faculty welcome the opportunity to advise honors students, for we imagine them to be like us, or like the students we believe we once were. It comes as a surprise to some faculty, therefore, that many honors students do not persist to graduation at a given institution. The reasons for the attrition differ, of course, from those of their less talented classmates. A sense of having chosen the wrong institution, a lack of compatible peers, or an unchallenging intellectual experience often proves to be the reason for the withdrawal of good students.

Honors students often come to college with high expectations. Some envision that their lives will now be lived on a different intellectual plane, with provocative classes, heady conversations with faculty, and stimulating encounters with peers. Reality often imposes a different picture, and the disappointment of honors students in college life can be immediate and intense. Having heard for years, "wait until you get to college," honors students may find it "just like high school" and may soon conclude that they chose the wrong institution or that college itself is overrated.

While increasing numbers of honors students anticipate continuing their education beyond the baccalaureate degree, some have difficulty in developing any plan for their future because they are confused by their many options. Other honors students are perfectionists and may be as devastated by a grade of B as other students are by an F. One large institutional study found that honors students were more likely than others to come from homes in which both parents had college or graduate degrees (Gerrity, Lawrence, and Sedlacek, 1993). For reasons of background as well as talent, they were more interested than were nonhonors students not just in preparing for graduate school, but also in learning. More surprising is the finding of this study that the honors students were more interested than others in campus life—student clubs and other activities.

These and other studies of honors students should alert faculty not to take the adjustment of their honors students for granted. Honors programs that connect honors students and offer them challenging courses, particularly in the freshman and sophomore years, help to shape college life to match more closely with what these students anticipate.

Advisers can also serve honors students by helping them conceptualize their undergraduate years in the broadest possible terms. The rapid expansion of knowledge, breaking down of disciplinary boundaries, and the accelerating rate of change should challenge our best students to seek a variety of experiences and to develop their skills and broad areas of knowledge to the greatest extent possible. We also serve our honor students well if we encourage them to master another language, study abroad, participate in research opportunities with faculty, and serve as learning mentors to their peers.

Whether on probation or receiving honors, today's students need competent, caring advisers who understand their needs as individuals and as members of special populations of students. Even more than earlier generations of students, they need thoughtful guidance and assistance, concern for fostering their learning, and help in making all of the many possibilities of the institution become actual for them. They also need faculty who will advocate for them, for their differences in backgrounds, learning styles, expectations of college life, and dreams for their futures. These faculty need to recognize that teaching, learning, and advising are interconnected and of critical significance to all of our undergraduates.

References

Association of American Colleges, Task Group on General Education. *A New Vitality in General Education.* Washington, D.C.: Association of American Colleges, 1988.

Astin, A. W. *What Matters in College?: Four Critical Years Revisited.* San Francisco: Jossey-Bass, 1993.

Chronicle of Higher Education. "The American Freshman: National Norms for Fall 1992." [American Council on Education and University of California Los Angeles Higher Education Research Institute], Jan. 13, 1993, A29–A33.

Cohen, J. "The Learning Disabled University Student: Signs and Initial Screening." *NASPA Journal,* 1984, 23–31.

Erickson, B. L., and Strommer, D. W. *Teaching College Freshmen.* San Francisco: Jossey-Bass, 1991.

Gerrity, D. A., Lawrence, J. F., and Sedlacek, W. E. "Honors and Nonhonors Freshmen: Demographics, Attitudes, Interests, and Behaviors." *NACADA Journal,* 1993, *13,* 43–52.

Goodsell, A. S., Maher, M. R., and Tinto, V. *Collaborative Learning: A Sourcebook for Higher Education.* University Park, PA: National Center on Postsecondary Teaching, Learning, and Assessment, 1992.

Green, M. F. (ed.). *Minorities on Campus: A Handbook for Enhancing Diversity.* Washington, D.C.: American Council on Education, 1989.

Habley, W. R. *Fulfilling the Promise? Final Report: ACT Fourth National Survey of Academic Advising.* Iowa City, Iowa: American College Testing, 1993.

Hall, R. M., and Sandler, B. R. "The Classroom Climate: A Chilly One for Women?" Reports on Women in Higher Education. Washington, D.C.: Association of American Colleges and Universities, 1982.

Johnson, D. W., Johnson, R. T., and Smith, K. A. *Cooperative Learning: Increasing College Faculty Instructional Productivity.* ASHE–ERIC Higher Education Report, no. 4. Washington, D.C.: George Washington University, School of Education and Human Development, 1991.

Levine, A. "The Making of a Generation." *Change,* Sept–Oct. 1993, 8–15.

Pascarella, E. T., and Terenzini, P. T. *How College Affects Students: Findings and Insights from Twenty Years of Research.* San Francisco: Jossey-Bass, 1991.

Schroeder, C. C. "New Students—New Learning Styles." *Change,* Sept–Oct. 1993, 21–26.

Terenzini, P. T. *The Transition to College: Easing the Passage.* University Park, PA: National Center on Postsecondary Teaching, Learning, and Assessment, 1993.

DIANE W. STROMMER is dean of University College and Special Academic Programs at the University of Rhode Island and the co-author of Teaching College Freshmen *(Jossey-Bass, 1991).*

Faculty should regard advising as an extension of the teaching role. However, they need more general institutional information and training if they are to perform effectively as teacher-advisers. Suggestions for formal and informal faculty advising development are made and three key elements in adviser preparation are identified.

Professional Development and Training for Faculty Advisers

Carol C. Ryan

According to the most recent survey on academic advising at accredited two- and four-year institutions across the country (American College Testing Program, 1992), 98 percent of all instructional faculty in departments serve as academic advisers to students. However, we have received little preparation in graduate school for this responsibility, and, at the majority of institutions surveyed by ACT, the only training or developmental assistance given to faculty is a one-day or half-day workshop each year. This presentation generally takes place in the fall and deals with institutional policies and procedures or changes in curriculum requirements.

Although many of us have had considerable advising experience, academic advising for the faculty member is more complicated than it was ten or fifteen years ago. The curriculum is more complex and students have more choices to make regarding programs, majors, and courses. Furthermore, the students we now advise are increasingly diverse in terms of age, ethnicity, and preparation for college work. Many are first-generation college-goers who need some clarification from us as to the mission or purpose of the university and what will be expected of them while they are there. We have also learned that we should advise students developmentally, or more holistically. We must take into account individual skills, abilities, and interests as we encourage advisees to set personal and career or vocational goals. We must continually collaborate with them as they develop educational plans to meet those goals.

The Role of the Faculty Adviser

Faculty are generally most interested in and knowledgeable about the institution's curriculum, particularly about those offerings in our own disciplines, departments, or colleges. Thus, much of what we do as advisers is to provide information about these topics. Students believe they will receive the most accurate information about programs, majors, and specific courses from us; and they are probably satisfied with this aspect of our relationship.

However, other questions arise from discussions with students about the curriculum. We need to be prepared to talk about the connections between disciplines or courses and also to discuss why certain courses are part of general education or core requirements or why other foundation work may be necessary for them. Some advisees are undecided about the choice of major. Others may take several introductory courses in a field and may discover that this area is not what they want to pursue after all. Still another group will not be able to enter the field of their choice and will come to us for assistance; and some have the ability to succeed in a particular discipline but need additional academic preparation before they can continue. Career options are an additional and important topic students want to discuss with faculty advisers; however, it is not an area in which we are particularly well-versed. Most of our graduates are not going on to graduate school or do not plan to teach. We must be prepared to talk with them about the types of careers other graduates in their field have followed or be able to refer them to an institutional resource where they can obtain current career information.

Professional Development for the Faculty Adviser

Faculty should regard the task of academic advising as an extension of the teaching role. Good academic advising requires that we establish a positive, open, and active learning environment in our office meetings with students and that we use our strongest classroom questioning and listening skills in the one-to-one teaching, or advising, session. Similarly, we can adapt teaching methods from our discipline to the advising setting, helping students make better educational and personal decisions by discussing with them, in a general way, some of the steps to take in problem-solving. These steps include information-gathering, analysis, review of alternatives, and seeking out the best possible solutions. We might even ask students to complete advising assignments, sending them off to appropriate institutional or community resources and asking them to bring back the results of their research at the next meeting. The research might lead to a choice of major or might require the student to search for acceptable alternatives to a major that the student is unable to enter.

It is helpful to consider the parallels between what we do in the classroom and in the advising setting. However, since faculty advisers are expected to respond to such a wide range of institutional concerns students bring, it is essential that we gain more broadly based institutional information and advising expertise. If our colleges or universities do not offer a comprehensive adviser-training program or we wish to learn more, we can build on our own skills and knowledge through readings, discussions with others, and attendance at workshops or seminars offered in other divisions at the institution. In the long run, such preparation will make us more effective and efficient as adviser-teachers, and students will derive more benefits from our work with them.

Three Key Elements in Faculty Adviser Preparation

Most practitioners and theorists in the field of academic advising believe that there are three key content areas (conceptual, informational, and relational) that faculty should address if they wish to improve their advising skills and knowledge. In this section, each area will be discussed; formal and informal methods by which the faculty adviser can obtain the information or practice the skills will be suggested.

Conceptual Understanding of Student Development. As we work individually with advisees, it can be useful to relate our understanding of human development theories to the issues, questions, and concerns the student presents. A basic understanding of the developmental tasks students are undertaking helps us as we work together to find the best courses of study and co-curricular activities that fit the advisee's interests and aspirations. Such knowledge enables us to accept the students as they are at that moment and to understand why an advisee's goals change, sometimes from one visit to the next.

A study of student development theorists, such as Chickering (1969), Perry (1970), Kohlberg (1981), and Gilligan (1982), provides insights into the predictable stages students move through. Faculty could read these theorists on their own or could invite another faculty member from the psychology or counseling department to speak at department or college meetings about the theories. Some knowledge of adult development theory is also important since so many of the students currently enrolled in public colleges or universities are over age twenty-five. Similarly, stage theories have been proposed in the field of vocational or career development. The faculty adviser who is interested in this topic could read Super (1980) or Holland (1985) or could talk with a career counselor at the institution about stages of career development as they interpret them. Again, another faculty member from the counseling or psychology department might speak on these topics at a unit meeting.

In addition, we need to educate ourselves about the particular cultural differences we may encounter as we advise students from backgrounds different than our own. We need to become better listeners and have a keener understanding of the issues such students may confront at our school. Most institutions provide workshops through college multicultural centers, international centers, or specific programs such as Native American Studies that help a faculty member gain a better understanding of the student's experience.

Some universities are also beginning to issue written materials that can serve as valuable resources for describing special student populations.

For the faculty adviser who wants to learn more about the conceptual framework of the advising process itself, O'Banion's five-step developmental advising model is the most widely accepted and practiced method (1972). The five steps include (1) exploration of life goals, (2) exploration of vocational goals, (3) program choice, (4) course choice, and (5) scheduling courses. The model provides a good structure for the advising interview with a student since it moves beyond routine information exchanges and requires that we ask questions first about personal goals and then about vocational and life choices. O'Banion's seminal article describing the model could be acquired through the school library. The adviser could read and practice the steps, or, better yet, discuss the model with other colleagues and work on questions for each step that best fits the program or discipline in which each is working with students. Another excellent resource on advising concepts and practices is the National Academic Advising Association's *NACADA Journal*. This publication, too, can be ordered through the school's library.

Institutional and Curricular Information. Since the curriculum and, in particular, our own discipline or subject, is what we know best, it is not difficult to share our knowledge with students in this area. However, it may be necessary to suggest that some time be set aside at college or departmental meetings, on a regular basis, to discuss changes in course or program requirements. Discussion with faculty members in departments where students must complete additional work that complements the major would also enrich an adviser's understanding of what the student can achieve.

If they have not already done so, faculty advisers should take some time to think about their own personal philosophy of higher education and about the reasons why they generally require a broad-based liberal arts foundation before students move into specific fields of study. Often, the connections between general education and the student's ultimate choice of major are not clear to advisees. If we cannot articulate our own understanding of these relationships and what a university education can be, it makes it more difficult for most students to discern the reasons behind requirements and to make sound educational decisions.

The faculty adviser must also acquire and share current information on university, college, or departmental regulations, policies, and procedures that affect students. The catalogue, student handbook, and department or college materials should provide most of the background information needed so that the adviser can accurately apprise students about options. A thorough understanding of the school's general education requirements is also a necessity. Some review of changes in admissions requirements into the major or new regulations or policies that affect these students with whom we work can be provided at department meetings on a regular basis. However, personal reading of the materials followed by informal discussions with contacts in the registrar's office, student affairs office, or advising offices provide answers to questions advisers might have. Students want to receive specific and accurate information from their advisers, and it is important that we either have the answers or that we know where to get them.

Effective faculty advisers should also have some knowledge of the co-curricular activities available to their advisees. Would the marketing or poetry club be a good experience for a particular student? Does the adviser know a student services professional who can talk about options such as internships or community service opportunities with advisees? Perhaps the student has confessed to poor study skills or the adviser and student have agreed that supplemental work is needed in mathematics. The adviser must be familiar with academic resources so as to refer students most appropriately. Sometimes student services program personnel offer workshops on these and other topics. The school may have programs for working with special populations. Faculty should cross the line and attend the sessions or ask that such sessions be repeated for a larger group of faculty in order to improve advising skills and knowledge.

Providing career information to advisees without some accumulation of current information on careers in the faculty member's area of expertise is difficult. Advisers or other personnel in the department should try to learn more and should share information about the jobs that graduates in their fields have taken. Questionnaires sent to graduates are often useful sources, and even newspaper and magazine accounts provide some information. A panel of alumni or community business people might also talk with faculty and students about careers and future job expectations. The adviser should call on the career development office at the school and should refer students to that resource; in some cases, the faculty member should go so far as to give an assignment to the advisee to come to the next appointment with information about specific careers. Since, on most campuses, this center also serves as an essential resource for students who are undecided about career directions or who are choosing or changing majors, the faculty adviser should be reasonably knowledgeable about the program's services and effectiveness.

Other information specific to advising that the faculty adviser should seek out includes the university's mission and policy on academic advising, if there is one. This document can give advisers a better sense of what is expected of them; it often includes a section on expectations for students. A presentation or written report on student retention at the institution is also helpful in assessing one's own responsibilities as an adviser. Faculty should acquire basic information on legal issues in advising. They should be aware of the Family Educational Rights and Privacy Act (1974) on keeping adviser records. Nothing should go into the records that an adviser would not be able to show the advisee or that would not be appropriate should the records be required by a court. The school's legal counsel could give a workshop on advising issues or could be asked to provide a written summary of pertinent information.

Finally, if a handbook for advisers is not provided, the faculty adviser should assemble the most important written materials she has identified and should organize the advising resources in a looseleaf notebook. The first page, for example, could be a current listing of college or university resources with names and telephone numbers of contacts for both the adviser and the student.

Relational Skills and Knowledge. Most of the relational, or communications, skills we use in the classroom are equally applicable in the advising setting. We should strive to create a welcoming, nonjudgmental atmosphere in our meetings with advisees so that they will feel free to consider new ideas, discard old ones, and raise questions or concerns. Using the open-ended and probing questions we have practiced as teachers, we can encourage and challenge advisees to think seriously about what they are learning, what they want to learn, and about the choices they will make. We can also transfer our active classroom listening skills to the advising meeting (what is the student really trying to tell us?), listening carefully and reflecting back what we think we hear. This allows students to clarify their ideas and to restate or reformulate their concerns.

We should also serve as role models for students, sharing our own academic or research interests and talking with them about what it means to be an educated person. In addition, we should take time to discuss what goes on in an academic community. Students are often initially astonished about the variety of views expressed and at the continuous questioning process that takes place within and between disciplines. They need to hear from us that this is one of the functions of the academy and they need to learn, too, how they can participate in the dialogues.

Students respond more positively in the classroom when instructors are enthusiastic about their subjects. This is also the case in the advising setting. If faculty advisers genuinely like to work with students and can communicate that feeling in advising, as well as showing some enthusiasm for their fields or for the university as a whole, students will be more likely to participate actively in the advising process and will also become more willing to take some chances, such as tackling new areas of learning.

Since, as teachers, we generally possess strong relational skills, less work in advising may be needed in this area. However, if advisers wish to learn more, workshops could be provided either by communications or education faculty. The adviser might also consciously decide to practice one or two relational skills, such as asking open-ended questions, during advising sessions. Another method is for two advisers to mentor each other, meeting monthly to exchange advising information and to talk about the relational aspects of their own advising practice. They might also work together to formulate general advising questions they could ask advisees, using the O'Banion model. For example, they might agree to ask new or undecided students open-ended questions about the subjects they have liked best, either in high school or college, or might work on questions that give students opportunities to talk about their interests, about concerns they have in certain subject areas, or about areas where they feel they need some help.

Outcomes of Adviser Development and Training

The strengths of faculty advisers lie in our understanding of our discipline areas and the requirements for study in that field. Students look to us to share that information as well as to receive general information about the broader curriculum and activities and services at the institution. Our role is to focus on the intellectual and social development of students, encouraging and challenging them to set life and career goals and to engage in educational planning that will help them reach those goals. However, we need more information than is presently provided if we are to function effectively in this way.

Since most of our institutions offer little formal adviser training beyond a single information workshop, faculty must find ways to learn more about academic advising and the conceptual, informational, and relational skills and knowledge needed to facilitate authentic one-to-one advising and teaching exchanges. Through readings, workshops offered at the institution, acquisition of information about other students resources, and informal discussions or pairing with other advisers, faculty members can build on their own skills and knowledge. If we begin to think about advising as a developmental process and try to apply our new knowledge as well as our teaching skills to the advising encounter, we will reap positive benefits. Because of the current and accurate information we have to share and our understanding of student development, advising may turn out to take less time. However, because of our new emphasis on the developmental and relational aspects of the advising exchange, contacts will become more productive and rewarding for both faculty and students.

With training, faculty will become better acquainted with students and will gain a clearer understanding of the strengths, limitations, hopes, and concerns they bring to the institution. As advisers, we will be able to assist students as they move through stages of development. Our advisees will be more likely to persist and succeed at the school because, as institutional representatives, we have taken an interest in them and their progress and have helped them make important decisions about their lives and their educational goals.

References

Chickering, A. *Education and Identity*. San Francisco: Jossey-Bass, 1969.

Gilligan, C. *In a Different Voice: Psychological Theory and Women's Development*. Cambridge, Mass: Harvard University Press, 1982.

Habley, W. R. *Fulfilling the Promise? Final Report, National Survey of Academic Advising*. Iowa City, Iowa: American College Testing Program, 1992.

Holland, J. *Making Vocational Choices*. Englewood Cliffs, N.J.: Prentice Hall, 1985.

Kohlberg, L. *The Philosophy of Moral Development*. New York: HarperCollins, 1981.

O'Banion, T. "An Academic Advising Model." *Junior College Journal*, 1972, 42, 62–69.

Perry, W. G., Jr. *Intellectual and Ethical Development in the College Years*. New York: Holt, Rinehart and Winston, 1970.

Super, D. "A Life-Span, Life-Space Approach to Career Development." *Journal of Vocational Behavior*, 1980, 16, 282–298.

CAROL C. RYAN has been associate professor in the College of Liberal Arts and currently serves as interim dean in the First College and coordinator for university academic advising at Metropolitan State University, Minneapolis/St. Paul, Minnesota. She is past president of the National Academic Advising Association.

*Advising students in the arts is a difficult and often perplexing task
that is being complicated by the realities of change both within and
outside higher education. While there are no easy solutions or answers
for the arts adviser, there are principles and philosophic viewpoints
that can help to make the process of advising more profitable and
honest both for the adviser and the student.*

Advising in the Arts: Some Thoughts and Observations for Arts Advisers

William J. Kelly

The creation and practice of art is a mysterious and profoundly individual act
of human expression. It combines skill and a command of technique with
deeply personal feelings, intuition, experimentation, blind faith, and, occasionally, dumb luck to bring works of art into being. Even then, the process of
art seldom yields success and, even less frequently, reward. Art is unpredictable
as an act and even more unpredictable as a vocation. The determination of
ability is a terribly subjective judgment, and the recognition of talent is always
far easier after the fact of achievement than before. In short, almost everything
about art is elusive and ephemeral; little about it can be traced or determined
with objective certainty.

   As a consequence, the teaching and mastery of art is a far different propo-
sition than, say, learning history or understanding the laws of physics. To the
adviser who must guide and counsel a student with an arts interest, the entire
process of advising is an extremely difficult task, often as mysterious and
daunting as the process of making art itself. The rules and regulations that
seem to work for most other forms of human enterprise do not seem to apply
to the arts. Even the answer to that most fundamental question—"Should I
consider pursuing an interest or career in the arts?"—can be very difficult to
arrive at and nearly impossible to determine with any degree of certainty. To
compound the adviser's problems, the world of art is changing in extraordinary ways and is rapidly altering our most basic conceptions of what art is and
how students should approach their training and education.

   I have been an arts adviser for over twenty years and find advising students to be as difficult now as when I first began. I know of no reasonable

means to determine talent and am increasingly unsure of the advisability or logic in encouraging students to pursue careers in the arts. I am equally unsure of the logic of discouraging students because in the arts the exception is, frequently, the rule and I have no way of accurately predicting whether a student will prove to be an exception or not. I have also grown to be very wary of rigid programmatic approaches to training and tend to view any program that claims to be "among the best" with deep suspicion. At present, there is very little assessment data available for arts training programs, especially in terms of outcomes, so most claims of excellence are made without much objective support. Even if objective measures could be cited, the merit of a particular program for a specific individual would still be a rather questionable matter, for the effect on an individual cannot be reasonably determined by looking at the effect on the general. The cultivating of an individual's talent and ability is always a terribly personal and unique situation that may have no relationship to the relative success or failure with others.

While I have built a healthy distrust for almost anything that appears to be absolute or assured in the advising of arts students, I have gained a respect for certain broad principles in advising that, I believe, are not only helpful but are also fundamental to the integrity of the process. I believe that in the arts, the central qualities of good advising reside in an acceptance of the student as an individual, a respect for honesty and the truth in all aspects of advising, and the adoption of an open-minded approach in dealing with any student. Unfortunately, this means admitting that there are no sure answers. One must rely on intuition and experience to a far greater degree than may be comfortable for many advisers, and one becomes far more knowledgeable about our students and their programs than many advisers see as possible given the constraints of already overcrowded schedules and ever-mounting responsibilities. But arts advising can never be reduced to easy formulas or be approached through the abstracted construct of a procedural process. There are simply too many variables and subtle influences that have bearing on the progress and growth of an individual student to address their needs adequately through prescriptive and mechanical means. Good advising is, therefore, personal, intuitive, and must proceed from trust . . . which must be earned and never taken for granted.

The principles that follow are neither formulas for success nor rules that should be followed as though they have the force of law. They are ideas and opinions that, I believe, have bearing and application in the process of advising arts students. As ideas and opinions, they exist only to guide and inform the process. In a sense, they are proposed to "advise the adviser." It is hoped that they will give those of us who work with arts students something to think about and consider.

PRINCIPLE 1. *Always be totally honest with students and make sure that they understand their arts interest as completely as possible.*

Above all, students, especially those who are contemplating careers in the arts, need to be advised in an honest, complete, and forthright manner. This means not only providing them with information that is true and accurate but also making them aware of the broad and specific implications of their possible decisions. Students should be helped to understand the fundamental truths that have bearing on whatever decisions they may eventually make. Far too often, it is presumed that students have a knowledge and understanding of their possible career paths, training options, and the educational opportunities that are available to them when, in reality, they have only the barest idea of what arts study may entail or what it may lead to. Most students actually know very little about the art that they are interested in or its process; they know even less about the realities of its professional practice. Their sense of art is all too commonly shaped by a myriad of half-truths, gross misconceptions, and romantic ideas about what a life in art will be like and demand of them.

It must always be remembered that most students come to the arts quite late in their academic careers and have very little background or experience in the field of art that has captured their interest. Most secondary schools have provided them with only limited exposure to the arts and have offered very little preparation or information about eventual careers in the arts. In a similar vein, most communities have relatively few working artists in them and, as a consequence, students have not been presented with reasonable models to learn from or gain a realistic view of professional practice. Instead, students' conceptions of working artists come primarily from those exalted few who have gained fame, national celebrity, and public exposure through the mass media. While students may know, intellectually, that "star" artists make up only a tiny minority in the world of art, it is through these artists' lives and achievements that most perceptions about art and artists are formed. And the romance of fame, wealth, and celebrity can be terribly compelling to a young person, especially in the absence of any other models.

There is, of course, an inherent value in seeing art as a romantic adventure and in building illusions that become more "real" than reality. In a sense, that is what a life in art is all about. But, from an advising perspective, most students have never been provided with any concrete information about or insight into the art of their interest. This makes it next to impossible for them to make informed decisions about what they should do. Bear in mind that their initial advising sessions are likely to be the first time that they will be afforded a realistic look at their interest. It is important that the adviser be knowledgeable, informed, and, above all, completely honest with them.

In the interest of honesty, there are certain realities of a life in art that, I believe, must be stressed for students. These "realities" may seem self-evident and obvious, but they are seldom given the attention and focus that they deserve. Students should ponder these realities and carefully weigh them against their desire, commitment, and dedication to pursuing their interest. Sooner or later, they will confront them and it is best that they do so at the earliest possible point in their career planning.

REALITY 1. *Many are called but few are chosen.*

A central reality of art in our culture and society is that it exists in a market environment and is subject to the laws of supply and demand like any other enterprise where goods are sold or services rendered. The reality of *all* areas of art is that supply dramatically exceeds demand in a proportion that is, likely, greater than in almost any other area of human endeavor. Far more books are written than are ever published, and only a tiny percentage of those that are published ever become successful. Fewer than 5 percent of professional actors in America work often enough to support themselves solely by the practice of their art. Poets, painters, sculptors, and musicians face a *likelihood* that their work will never be recognized, let alone support them or provide them with any level of security. Fame, wealth, and celebrity in the arts come with about the same frequency as being struck by lightning or winning the lottery. If careers in the arts can be likened to anything, it is to professional sports; competition in the NBA or the NFL is not dramatically different than that which is faced by artists.

There are, of course, other measures of success in the arts than financial reward or personal recognition. Art provides artists with their say in the human debate. For many, the ability to express themselves in paint, words, clay, on a stage, or in front of a camera is reward in itself. But for the student, this is an important reality that must be faced squarely and seriously. I believe that advisers must ask students to constantly confront their passions about art and constantly re-examine the need for art in their lives. This does not mean surrendering their dreams, hopes, faith, or illusions to a mean and pragmatic view. On the contrary, this may mean surrendering themselves to their dreams and embracing their illusions as though they were absolute truths. But this is not something to be taken lightly. Art can be mercilessly demanding and can exact a heavy price from those who pursue it. Students must grapple with this and be prepared to grapple with it for the rest of their lives.

REALITY 2. *There is no substitute for talent.*

Most students who come to the arts have been told by someone at some point in their lives that they were "talented." As is true of fame and celebrity, the mere mention of talent can be intoxicating. It tells us that we are special, different, and gifted in ways that others are not. But "talent" is a terribly relative term that can never be objectified to the point where it will serve as a predictor of any outcome in an art. We may know "where our talents lie," but can never know if they will be enough or, ultimately, if they will see us through. There is also no known correlation between talent and success. About all that can reasonably be said about talent is that without it the artist has only luck to fall back on.

Most people who teach or work in the arts develop an instinct for talent and are, frequently, called upon to exercise that instinct in evaluating the potential or progress of students. Auditions, portfolio reviews, competitions, and even classroom performance are all guided, to some extent, by the perception of talent in the work of an individual. But it is important that students understand that talent is always a relative judgment and that it is always conditioned by the background and experience of the person who levels that judgment. The stories of students who were told that they "weren't talented enough" and then built careers and achievements that gave the lie to that assessment are commonplace in every discipline of art. More frequent, but seldom told, are the stories of students who were believed to possess vast stores of talent but were never able to make good on their promise or potential.

As an adviser, I think it is important that students recognize that estimations of their talent, held by themselves or others, are ultimately only opinions that do not carry the force of any objective truth. While there is clear value in the schooled instincts of those who have spent their lives watching and examining the progress of young artists, there is nothing in an adviser's or instructor's opinion, either positive or negative, that tells the student more than their reasoned estimation. As with most things in art, talent must be probed, questioned, encouraged, and challenged, but never thought of as fixed or immutable.

REALITY 3. *Failure is an essential truth in art, and art is built upon failure far more often than upon success.*

Artists need to be thick-skinned and need to possess the ability not only to bounce back from failure but also to thrive on it. Contrary to the images of success that we encounter in the media, most artists live with failure as the true constant in their lives. Beyond the obvious fact that few artists succeed in a public sense, there is the more powerful truth that the whole process of creation is rife with personal failure that seldom is made public and is always accompanied by blows to the ego that are painful and deeply felt. To bring a work to completion, the artist must wade through a mire of unsuccessful attempts, thwarted ideas, and potentials that are never realized. The despair of the color that cannot be mixed, the words and rhymes that cannot be found, and the note that remains constantly elusive are always present in the artist's life and, for those whose lives are devoted to art, the process of confronting that despair repeats again and again. Even work that "succeeds" is seldom as satisfying or rewarding to the artist as it is for the audience who embraces it without question: they have no idea what it might have been. And then there are the critics.

As an adviser, I think it is important to tell students that they must expect, accept, and learn to live with the reality of failure as a central fact in their lives. The fear of living without success is modest when compared to the reality of living with failure—a near certainty in any artist's life. The greatest obstacle that must be overcome in art comes in the confrontation of the inevitability of failure.

REALITY 4. *Making art is work and work is not play.*

Most students come to the arts out of a desire to turn an avocation into a vocation. But in the transfer of an avocational activity to a vocational pursuit something deep and profoundly different happens. There is always a thrill and a kind of ecstasy that comes with bringing something into existence out of one's own experience and skill. This is fundamental in art, but there is a powerful difference in doing that when moved or inspired and doing it on demand. Art, at least as a vocational calling, does not work well in fits and starts. It demands constant attention and often relentless pursuit. It calls for intense concentration and exertion of supreme will to overcome those blocks to creativity that rise up like demons to thwart the creative process. Things like "writer's block" and the confrontation of the empty canvas or the blank page are constant realities in the life of an artist that must be faced and, frequently, stared down if one is to move forward. The making of art can be richly rewarding and deeply satisfying, but it is never easy and seldom "fun."

As an adviser, I think it important to remind students that there is a profound difference between the experience of art in their lives and the experience of a life in art. To believe that a life in art is merely an expansion of an avocational interest is self-delusion on a grand scale. If a career is their objective, they must be prepared for everything to change and for that change to transform their lives. They must be prepared to enter the world of work and to abandon their fascination with play.

REALITY 5. *Experience is the best teacher.*

The unfortunate last reality of all is that these realities can only be understood in a meaningful way through actual experience. To talk about the realities of art in the abstract may be somewhat instructive but will seldom mean very much to a student who has not yet been touched by those darker aspects of art or life in general. Young people whose lives are being directed by dreams, ambition, and the anticipation of future accomplishment will seldom believe that the pain, frustrations, and disappointments of art will actually visit themselves upon them. They will see these things as realities but, almost always, as realities for someone else. What is important is that they store this information away and learn from it when the time comes; they need to learn about themselves and about their commitment to their art. Part of the adviser's role is to prepare them for the realities that will come and help them to understand that their character, as artists and individuals, will be formed out of adversity. As in most things, "whatever doesn't kill them will make them strong," and those that become strong will constitute our next generation of artists.

The basic need for honesty and a comprehensive look at the arts in the context of a student's preparation for study is, simply, to make sure that they know the full dimension of what their pursuit is likely to entail. The idea is neither to discourage nor encourage but merely to acquaint them with the truth. In a sense, the truth becomes a "leveler," an agent to bring all conceptions of art into balance, thereby allowing students to weigh their decisions in a more realistic environment. It is doubtful that mere honesty will alter or change the decisions that most students ultimately make, but honesty will begin an important process of examination and personal evaluation for them. As they gain experience and background, this process will become increasingly valuable. The most important decisions that students make will occur somewhere in their future. This process, if based in honesty, will serve as a guide and reference to help them when those important decisions must be made.

PRINCIPLE 2. *Students are individuals and, in the arts, it is the individual that is most important.*

Part of the problem in the current state of higher education is that almost everything that we do has become institutionalized, systematized, and preprogrammed to produce predictable and "desired" results. Our curricula are becoming increasingly standardized, prescriptive, and made credit-heavy in the process. Our models of excellence are with greater and greater frequency coming from the world of business and our daily lives are awash with business procedures, techniques, strategies, and methodologies. Good programs are now viewed as those that function like well-oiled machines and conform to the specifics that are set forth by accrediting bodies as though education were a matter of understanding the rules and playing by them without question or complaint. Good students are generally understood as those who are compliant, do what they are told, and work hard—rather like robots. Arts programs are, in this respect, no different from any other. They have become models of curricular design and "checksheet organization." Their strengths are measured in their mechanics and their benefits to students are expressed in programmatic terms.

But art and its creation is still a matter of individual insight, vision, and passion and is seldom produced by design or the conformance to any set plan or order. Art is also a rebellious act that proceeds, most frequently, from a desire to see things differently and to disturb whatever the balance is that has been struck at any particular point in our social or cultural history. Artists instinctively seek change and work to alter our perceptions. Their strengths lie in their idiosyncrasies and their variance with established order and convention. Given this fundamental truth of art, I, as an educator, have serious questions about the value and benefit of the intensely programmatic approaches that have become commonplace in arts education. I question whether regimented, inflexible, narrowly defined "learning paths" actually foster and school artists or if they may actually inhibit their growth and progress. More problematic is the fact that they engender a belief in our students that art can be learned by completing the required coursework and that "professional training" is a necessary prerequisite to creating art in the first place. Admittedly, these questions are more germane to a discussion of curricular reform than to one on advising, but they do relate to fundamental concerns in advising that need to be addressed.

The core concern is with the state of the individual in the now mechanized process of arts education and the all-too-frequent reality that individuals have been lost within the system that supposedly has been designed to serve them. Arts training, in many of our best institutions, has become a matter of plan, and the primary concern of most advisers is to make sure that their students conform to the plan. We know and advise our students through their checksheets. We see them not as individuals, or even people, but as collections of courses: requirements completed and requirements remaining to be fulfilled. Neither we nor they ask many questions that are not about those checksheets. There is no reason to do so. We both know that it is the checksheet that is important. The actual interests, aspirations, beliefs, and passions of the student seem outside of the process. And, as a consequence, the student as an individual, a unique and special person, is lost to us.

Clearly, this is wrong and antithetical to both the process of advising and to any reasonable understanding of training in an art. Surely, no plan is so perfect, universal, or absolute that it can be applied to all students without some recognition of their unique and personal attributes. Surely there are a multitude of variances, variables, and circumstances unique to the individual student that must upset and disturb the perfect balance of the plan. And, surely, it is far more important to determine how well the plan is serving the student than to determine how well the student is serving the plan.

The most common question posed to the adviser is "what should I take next semester?" With a fast review of the checksheet, the adviser can deliver an answer. I propose that the adviser cannot answer that question by referring to the checksheet or by reviewing the program plan for that student's interest. I contend that the question can only be reasonably answered by knowing the student as a unique individual and having some clear idea about what that particular student wants, needs, and desires from his or her education. We must take the time to get to know our advisees. We must ask them questions and we must question ourselves about them. We must try to find out what is working for them and what is not and then try to determine why particular aspects of their education succeed or fail. We must be willing and able to propose options and alternatives that address their particular needs and circumstances. And we must ask whether the particular program of study that the students are engaged in is really the best for them, their talents, and their sensibilities.

While the proliferation of programmatic approaches to arts training and the increased dependency on accreditation norms have created a more homogeneous picture of arts training in the United States, most programs still acquire a basic character and adopt a philosophic stance that distinguishes them from others. Typically, any program will serve some students very well but will achieve only modest success with others. And almost any program, no matter how well designed or conceived, will prove to be detrimental to some students. This, I believe, has very little to do with either the quality of the program or the potential of the student but, instead, is primarily a factor of the "mix." Advisers must develop a sensitivity for the chemistry of the "mix" and be cognizant of the effect of that mix on the individual. It is important that advisers not be unduly influenced by program loyalties and lose their objectivity in offering counsel to individual students. Advisers should see themselves as advocates for the best interests of their individual students and not as defenders or apologists for their programs. Advisers must stand aloof from the "plan" and concentrate their best energies on realizing the best in their students.

At times, the wisest counsel that can be offered to students is that they should seek a more profitable learning environment through transfer or program change. This, of course, means being knowledgeable about other programs and being sensitive to the particular needs, strengths, and backgrounds of individual advisees. Extreme care must be exercised in such situations so that students who do not benefit from a particular approach to training do not see themselves as failures or "misfits" in a negative sense but merely as individuals not fully benefiting from the approach that a program advocates. It would be best if this could be determined prior to enrollment, but, as with most factors in arts training, this will usually become apparent only through a process of trial and error.

A more difficult but no less frequent circumstance arises from the inevitable conflicts that emerge when an individual's desire for personal expression meets the rigidity of programmatic structures. It must be remembered that most students who come to the arts do so out of a desire to exploit their individuality and escape from structures that they feel inhibit them and force them into some kind of conformity. When they encounter such structures in their arts training, they often feel confused, angry, and, sometimes, betrayed. They may question, challenge, and even rebel against prescriptive structures and "cookie-cutter" approaches in their training. Rather than viewing them as "malcontents" or "difficult," advisers must come to understand and deal with them as individuals whose most basic drives naturally resist regimentation and constraint. If possible, accommodations should be sought and energies redirected to more profitable pursuits within the broad context of their training. Options for independent study or self-directed learning should be explored to give students greater opportunity to individualize their education. Special and unique alternatives to the established paths should be made available to reduce the sense of rigidity in programs. And secondary interests should be exploited to round out and expand students' learning potential. To force students to conform, to do "what is best for them" with no acknowledgment of their particular needs, can be terribly counterproductive both for the students and the program. It is wise to remember that the "best" student may well be the most problematic. Traits like compliance, accommodation, complaisance, and affability may be most appreciated in student-adviser relationships but seldom are traits that one would associate with the artistic temperament or character.

PRINCIPLE 3. *The world is changing rapidly and we must keep pace with change or risk preparing students for a world that no longer exits.*

The realities of a world that is becoming smaller, increasingly linked and driven by technology, and fundamentally different from the world of twenty-five years ago must be faced in the arts as in all other areas of higher education. As we stand on the doorstep of the twenty-first century, we see change that is already occurring with blinding speed and that promises to accelerate rather than diminish in the foreseeable future. New areas of art are opening up on a daily basis, and the older arts are fighting for their very survival or are being transformed in ways that make them almost unrecognizable to us. Even our most fundamental perceptions of art and its nature are being challenged and brought into question.

In the past decade, music has become an art no longer purely aural but profoundly visual in its practice. Students can look forward to a world where photographic film will be replaced by digital floppy disks and the darkroom will become as peculiar an artifact of the past as the phonograph record. "Paint" will increasingly mean color pixels bound by an electronic glue rather than pigment suspended in a more material medium. Even the written word is being transformed by "multi-media authoring." Sound and images may become as common a fixture in fiction and poetry as chapter and verse are today. And the "convergence of media" will give rise to new arts that will make no distinction between sound, image, text, and motion in their creation. Technology is and will continue to alter the landscape of art and will likely make it almost unrecognizable by the standards of today . . . and will do so in a very short time.

As advisers, we must recognize that many of our students have already embraced this vision of the future as a reality in their lives. Their perception of art, careers in art, and training for those careers reaches far beyond the structures that are in place at virtually all of our institutions of higher learning. Many of these students see our arts colleges as peculiar anachronisms and are seeking new approaches and new paths that, by and large, do not yet exist. Rather than resist change or turn our backs on it, we must seek out new ways to accommodate these students. We must argue for the creation of new programs and approaches that accept interdisciplinary approaches and the linking of skills that would have been unthinkable in an arts context only a few years ago. Biomedical illustration, computer-based animation, special effects design, and the music video are but a few of the already established career fields that demand interdisciplinary study beyond the scope of most of our established programs. In a terribly pragmatic view, if we do not bend to the winds of change, we may become true anachronisms in our lifetime and fall by the wayside along the path of the new.

Beyond the call for fundamental change in our approaches to art within our colleges and universities, advisers must be prepared to seek out already existing structures that may accommodate the interests of special students. In many of our colleges and universities, there are interdisciplinary programs and options that may work for students whose interests cross over traditionally separate areas of endeavor. College-based advising centers must recognize these emerging interests and serve, at least in the interim, as resources for students who no longer conform to the established norms but may become our most valuable and productive artists in the future. And individual advisers must accept the fact that what has worked in the past may be irrelevant in the future. If we are truly to serve our students and the future that they will build, we must become far more flexible and forward-looking then we are now.

PRINCIPLE 4. *We are the gardeners for men.*

The role of the arts adviser is greater than that of a mere functionary to insure that procedures are followed and graduation credits are correctly audited. The arts adviser, through wise counsel, can help a student become a creator. The adviser has more at stake than students or their careers or the satisfaction of a job well done. What is at stake is art.

Just before the outbreak of World War II, Antoine de Saint Exupery sat in a train crowded with refugees fleeing the tyranny of Nazi Germany. There he encountered a peasant family hoping to find freedom or escape in those terrible days before Europe tumbled headlong into war. This encounter led to a meditation not on war or its suffering but on art and the fate of man outside of the realities of war:

> I sat down face to face with one couple. Between the man and the woman a child had hollowed himself out a place and fallen asleep. He turned in his slumber, and in the dim lamplight I saw his face. What an adorable face! A golden fruit had been born of these two peasants. Forth from this sluggish scum had sprung this miracle of delight and grace.
>
> I bent over the smooth brow, over those mildly pouting lips, and I said to myself: This is a musician's face. This is the child Mozart. This is a life full of beautiful promise. Little princes in legends are not different from this. Protected, sheltered, cultivated, what could not this child become?
>
> When by mutation a new rose is born in a garden, all the gardeners rejoice. They isolate the rose, tend it, foster it. But there is no gardener for men. This little Mozart will be shaped like the rest by the common stamping machine. This little Mozart will love shoddy music in the stench of night dives. This little Mozart is condemned.
>
> I went back to my sleeping car. I said to myself: their fate causes these people no suffering. It is not an impulse to charity that has upset me like this. I am not weeping over an eternally open wound. Those who carry the wound do not feel it. It is the human race and not the individual that is wounded here, is outraged here. I do not believe in pity. What torments me tonight is the gardener's point of view. What torments me tonight is not this poverty to which after all a man can accustom himself as easily as to sloth. . . . What torments me is not the humps nor hollows nor even the ugliness.

It is the sight, a little bit in all these men, of Mozart murdered (Saint Exupery, 1940, pp. 205–206).

Like Saint Exupery, I take the gardener's point of view. Like Saint Exupery, I fear the sight of Mozart murdered. But, unlike Saint Exupery, I do not believe that "there is no gardener for men." We, as teachers and advisers, are the gardeners for men. And if we fail, as I fear we often do, we become accomplices in the murder of these little Mozarts and play our part in the inevitable loss to the garden. If we are to protect the future, we must always be on guard against the "sins of neglect" and the loss of the rose. If art is to survive as a fact of consequence in the lives of men, we must do all that we can to make sure that the potential for art's future is "protected, sheltered, and cultivated" in our students for, ultimately, it is not their interest that is being served but ours.

Reference

Saint Exupery, A. de. *Wind, Sand, and Stars*. New York: Harcourt, Brace, 1940.

WILLIAM J. KELLY is associate professor of theatre and integrative arts at The Pennsylvania State University and professor-in-charge of the Department of Integrative Arts at the University Park Campus.

This chapter provides a practical guide to advising social science students based on the experiences of two social scientists, a sociologist and psychologist, each of whom has taught in both discipline-based and interdisciplinary departments.

Social Science Advising

Gilbert Geis, Ted L. Huston

The dean of the business school at a major university recently offered the following story of his experiences with academic advising during his undergraduate days. When he arrived on campus, he had to indicate what he would prefer to study, and decided that medicine seemed like a decent route for a young man who wanted to move up in the world. Two quarters later, as a premedical student, he was on academic probation and within painful sight of following his father into work in the coal mines. In desperation, he sought out a social science adviser his friends had told him might prove helpful.

The adviser invited him to the Student Union for a coke, listened to his tale of woe, and signed him up for the forthcoming quarter for a coterie of courses that would ease his transition into college. The common element in the classes selected was that each had the reputation for providing stimulating intellectual fare and for a grading policy that bore a close relationship to the amount of effort students put into their work. The faculty adviser also set up regular meetings with the student to monitor his progress. The meetings provided an opportunity for the adviser to offer suggestions about studying tactics, how to "read" a professor, how to prepare for exams, and similar hints that might ease the path of academic progress. The student was told, for instance, that it was a good idea to register for one more class than he planned to take, to sample all of the classes, and then to drop the one that appeared the least palatable. This last kind of advice, though it imposes costs and concerns from the perspective of the college or university bureaucracy, is based on a fundamental premise: that the university is not operated primarily in the service of professors and administrators. On the contrary, it is there to serve students. Institutional personnel often overlook this premise since they are entrenched and their clientele is transient.

The remainder of the story of the one-time premedical student is filled in easily enough. The student was encouraged to take a range of social science offerings, including anthropology, economics, psychology, and sociology, and to register in some courses in ancillary units traveling under such names as human ecology, communications, and social work. Unfortunately, fairly rigid requirements concerning the number of required courses necessary for graduation precluded an altogether satisfactory sampling of what might have been worthwhile undergraduate offerings in other social science fields.

In all, the route from struggling student to successful dean was marked by increasing success and competence. The underlying moral of the story is that advisers can have an enormous impact on the immediate personal and academic experiences of those with whom they work and on the quality of their entire lives.

Similar stories, of course, do not always have happy endings, and sometimes an adviser has to accept the considerable responsibility of determining whether a student is capable, possesses the motivation, and for other reasons deserves to be coddled a bit. Advising is time-consuming and energy-draining. Perhaps the first rule is that, as a resource, it should not be expended carelessly and inefficiently.

Gathering Data on Advising

Altogether too little attention has been paid to whether a particular adviser is the best one for a particular student. This topic alone would lend itself to social science research. It may well be that the commitment of the adviser is the critical factor in whether the relationship proves to be valuable. Students commonly complain that they did not hit it off with their adviser, and that the relationship was formal and perfunctory. But they are often shy about changing advisers. They assume that the one they were given is by some divine decree the one with whom they must remain. They also tend to have a vague apprehension that something dire will happen if they turn their back on their assigned adviser, that he or she will be angry with them. Advisers ought to be perfectly willing to encourage any student shift to a different adviser if they believe that the result will be productive, be it a matter of personality or shared interests. It is arguable whether students ought to be gender-matched with advisers, and the truth probably is that it is a good idea for some to work with same-sex advisers and that it is disadvantageous for others.

Faculty advisers, like judges, psychiatrists, and others who provide advice and make decisions about others' lives, usually remain astonishingly unaware of the results of their intervention. Anecdotal evidence inevitably trickles back, but there is the human tendency to remember the successes and put out of mind the failures. Unlike medical doctors, social science advisers cannot bury their mistakes; on the other hand, some of us at least are fortunate indeed that we are not as beset with suits for malpractice for incorrect information or bad advice.

On an informal level, it might be a good idea—and fun—to keep a record of predictions of the outcome of advice that is offered students. This evaluation would determine whether you are operating in terms of folklore and instinct or whether you can derive some empirical evidence to support what you do as an adviser. Of course, you will also discover that much of your advice is ignored and that, as many advisers sooner or later find out, much of what is presented as a quest for advice is rather an attempt to locate support for a predetermined and irrevocable decision.

Those with a zest for such things could launch more formidable research experiments to determine the consequences of different forms and elements of advising. This is an important area that needs satisfactory research. Such work inevitably must be limited by the reasonable human subjects imperative that you cannot withhold what seem to be worthwhile services from one person and offer them to another only to determine whether they truly work. But, to take the matter mentioned earlier, it ought to be relatively easy to determine—from the viewpoint of both the mentor and the advisee—which kinds of persons show the greatest rapport in same-gender and different-gender advising situations and how this rapport, in turn, bears upon the quality of advice given and its likelihood of being absorbed by the student.

Helping Students Choose a Major

An early concern is to determine whether students who come for advice belong in the majors they have declared. Students on most campuses change majors at least once during their college career (Gordon, 1984). We know of no study that convincingly portrays why particular students select particular majors—both those who succeed and those who do less well—though there is post facto anecdotal evidence galore concerning what originally drew successful people to their choice of work. For instance, Edwin H. Sutherland, probably America's foremost criminologist, notes how he was influenced to choose sociology as his major by Charles Henderson, his teacher at the University of Chicago:

> When I entered Dr. Henderson's course, I received personal attention. He spoke to me, knew me, was interested in me. Consequently, I was interested in pursuing sociology and interested in the type of sociology Dr. Henderson presented (Geis and Goff, 1983, p. xxiv).

For other statements concerning the influences that led people to pursue the social sciences, see the autobiographies of Margaret Mead (1972) and B. F. Skinner (1976), as well as studies by Joseph Dorfman on Thorsten Veblen (1934), Alfred Marrow on Kurt Lewin (1969), and Irving Horowitz on C. Wright Mills (1983). The influences of parents, high school teachers, and advisers undoubtedly are important factors; we suspect that chance and inertia also play a notable role in such decisions. This is another area that cries out for good research.

It is often startling to an adviser to find out how little a student knows about the field that he or she has chosen as a major. This does not mean, of course, that in time the student will not come to find fulfillment in the discipline. One of the present writers thought he was entering a clinical psychology preparatory program and was distressed on arrival to learn that the emphasis in the department was on academic psychology, not clinical practice. Today, he cannot imagine how he could have considered being a clinician, and praises constantly those who inspired his interest in academic psychology generally and in social psychology more particularly.

Nonetheless, newcomers should immediately be informed about the field they prefer to study. It probably is a good idea to have printed materials available, beyond those that appear in the catalogue, portraying the career opportunities appropriate for a person who completes a major in that field. Even more valuable as a truth-in-advertising tactic will be a list of those who have graduated with majors in the subject during the past, perhaps, seven years, and a statement informing readers about how they are leading their lives currently. If a sufficient number of graduates are in the area or return to campus on occasion, it will be useful to have them discuss with majors in your field, and prospective majors, if possible, how they look back upon their own undergraduate experiences and what they recommend for current students.

Typically, students, especially those selecting sociology and psychology as their major, assert that they have done so because they "like to work with people" or they "want to do something important with their life." These kinds of statements almost invariably are offered with a bit more than necessary gregariousness or earnestness in order to demonstrate to you the unusual social concern of the advisee. Others, such as those professing an interest in pursuing law or medicine, often know little about these professions other than what they have seen on television—and what they have heard about their lucrativeness.

Gentle probes should help to penetrate beneath commonplace clichés and to force the student to define with greater precision what it is that is desired from the chosen academic major and from the anticipated work of a lifetime. It is often worthwhile to point out with some emphasis that advancement in many jobs typically involves less and less direct contact with people, such as clients, and deeper involvement in desk-bound management chores. The newspaper reporter rises to office-based editor, the social worker to supervisor.

Of course, clinical psychologists and other counselors—positions highly attractive to college students—continue to deal throughout their careers with people in need of their help. Here a student might be warned that the pleasure of offering interpretation or encouraging clients or patients to work out their problems both have a tendency to pall with time. The presenting problems may prove monotonously repetitive or essentially intractable. Students should be made aware that some occupations engender a high degree of burnout.

Other occupations that are likely to be chosen by social science majors have advantages and demerits that often are not obvious to college students.

The foreign service, for example, which seems like nirvana to some political science majors, has a grueling up-or-out promotion system, with fewer and fewer people able to advance beyond a certain point; those who choose this field are often forced to abandon their careers at a relatively early age. College and university teaching, by contrast, has room at the top for anybody who can meet what are relatively achievable standards. Political science majors, of course, in considerable numbers desire to prepare themselves for careers in law. An adviser might want to point out the rather high level of disenchantment that often arises among practicing lawyers a few years down the line. Young lawyers with fine academic records and law review editorships at good law schools usually earn very substantial salaries, but they work extremely long hours and often at tasks a good deal less glamorous than those portrayed on television. The practice of law often has more to do with the preparation and careful proofing of briefs and other legal documents than it does with the courtroom. Persons unaccustomed to adversarial stances can find constant legal quarrels irksome and difficult to deal with effectively. In addition, while ample support exists in the ethical codes, some students will inevitably find it unsavory to be advocating positions that they know are morally wrong, however successful they may be in having them declared the winning side in a court of law.

Internships

Many college and universities have found it worthwhile to offer for credit field placements in social agencies, law firms, and businesses in the community. Students very often regard these as one of the highlights of their undergraduate experience. They are, often for the first time, able to see the practical implications of classroom learning and, if nothing else, they gain a feeling of being adult. Some inevitably will come to find jobs in places where they have interned as part of their educational experience; others will be appalled at how little they appreciated the negative qualities of the work they had contemplated doing. For the adviser, a major consideration is to make certain that the placement represents a true learning experience and not busy gofer work.

Preparing Students for Graduate and Professional Schools

For social science majors who intend to go on to graduate school, and for aspiring lawyers or doctors who plan to pursue graduate work in professional schools, there exists a serious question concerning whether the best preparation for such a lifetime of work in a field lies within that field itself. On the positive side, a strong argument can be made that a student ought to be exposed sufficiently to a discipline so that he or she can reasonably determine whether it actually holds the appeal it had been presumed to have. In addition, early learning gives the student grounding that can allow ready forward movement in graduate or professional school.

In this regard, we would strongly recommend that undergraduate students contemplating advanced degrees be encouraged during their last two years to try to do some research work of a publishable quality. Typically, the easiest way to get into print is to carry out a questionnaire study that provides data on a controversial or important issue. One of the authors, for instance, taught an undergraduate seminar in which three of the ten submitted papers were ultimately published. In one, as an example, the student, having been told that Minnesota was the only state that allowed defense attorneys to have the last word to the jury, reviewed what communications and social psychology research had to say about the advantages and disadvantages of such a format, sent questionnaires to a sample of defense attorneys and all of the prosecutors in the state requesting their answer to a series of questions about the practice, and dug a bit into the views of jurisprudence in continental Europe, where the same practice prevails. The article was accepted in the *Minnesota Law Review,* and has subsequently been quoted in several state Supreme Court decisions.

But this leaves still unresolved the question of whether those contemplating a career in a social science ought to major in the field as undergraduates. One of the earliest and very best books that surveyed the later reactions of persons to their undergraduate experiences—*They Went to College: The College Graduate in America Today* by Ernest Havemann and Patricia West—found them very enthusiastic about their time as students. Some, however, were a bit disenchanted by the fact that they had not dipped more into areas in which they would not spend the rest of their lives. It was music, literature, and art that they yearned for: they sometimes regarded the time in preprofessional work as merely a repetition of what they would endlessly do on their jobs, and could have learned rapidly once they were on the job.

The systematic study of the impact of college on the life course has a long history. A 25-year longitudinal study of Bennington College carried out by Newcomb and his colleagues makes for particularly interesting reading (Newcomb, Koenig, Flacks, and Warwick, 1967). Two books, *The Impact of College on Students* (Feldman and Newcomb, 1969) and *How College Affects Students* (Pascarella and Terenzini, 1991) are recommended for those who wish to acquire a more in-depth understanding of the ways in which the college experience has an impact on students.

The advice Riesman (1973) gave his students at Radcliffe and Harvard echoes the views of these former students. He encouraged students to do the following:

> Take out career insurance against the chances and mischances of life, organizing their undergraduate years so that they emerge with the confidence born of competence, that if one track fails they can find another: having learned one language, they can more easily learn others, or learn other demanding skills that will open to still others (p. xx).

Riesman (1973) urged students to "employ their college years to learn a life-long sport, a lifelong musical instrument, and other lifelong interests that may stand them in good stead, whatever fate befalls them in later life" (p. xxi).

Besides the failure to locate interests as undergraduates that will provide for an exciting extravocational intellectual and esthetic adult playground, those who contemplate professional careers in academic or other kinds of professional work rarely appreciate the enormous demand for writing abilities. The most technically skilled scholars will find it difficult to move forward if they are unable to convey their ideas in grammatically sound, clear, and logical ways. There is much to be said for English as an undergraduate major in preparation for virtually any work in the social sciences. All students ought to be strongly encouraged to take a good deal of classwork to improve their writing skills. In that regard, social science departments ought to be generous, though the enrollment costs can be painful, in providing adequate elective options outside their own fields.

Since many social science-related careers require an advanced degree, advisers might want to help students early in their undergraduate career to understand what will be required of them if they hope to succeed in post-graduate work. Advisers should assiduously avoid seeking to clone themselves through students. It is often said that scientists seek disciples, while faculty in professional programs focus on helping students develop practical skills (Reisman, 1957). The successful adviser will need to know something about graduate programs that are not merely graduate extensions of their own undergraduate programs. A student interested in families and children, for example, ought to consider an array of types of graduate programs, including developmental psychology, sociology, interdisciplinary programs in child development and family studies, pediatrics or pediatric nursing, psychiatry, social work, child clinical psychology, school psychology, marriage and family counseling, public policy, and family law.

It is essential that social science advisers help students become knowledgeable about the character and the requirements for admission to the types of graduate programs that might be suited to their interests. Most graduate programs in the social sciences require students to take the Graduate Record Examination (GRE). Prelaw students should take a cram course for the LSAT (Law Schools Admissions Test), if at all possible, and take the test in a timely fashion.

The earlier that students learn how their relevant test performances and their grade point averages blend, the earlier they can figure out the statistical likelihood that they will be admitted to this or that graduate program or professional school. Undergraduates are often unaware that academically oriented graduate programs ordinarily are able to provide graduate assistantships that defray much, if not most, of the costs of pursuing a graduate education. The story is quite different with regard to professional schools, such as law school or medical school, where the expenses are largely borne by the student. It is best that students learn about these schools and programs for which they prove qualified as early as possible. Students should be encouraged to find out about the admissions criteria, test dates, costs, and the strengths and the weaknesses of various graduate programs. A good place to start is by writing to the national headquarters for the discipline. The addresses of four major social science disciplines are listed at the end of this chapter.[1]

Final Comments

Social science advisers generally are characterized and differentiated from advisers in other disciplines by their interest in human behavior. More than other advisers, they ought to use that interest to develop sophisticated research designs that identify the crucial ingredients of the successful adviser-advisee relationship. They also ought to seek to understand how best to match students' abilities with curricular and extracurricular opportunities. They should systematically identify what works and what does not work, with whom, and under what circumstances. One of life's most satisfying experiences is to have a well-advised student, ten or twenty years down the line, tell you how much you influenced his or her life for the better. Advising human beings can be a demanding, daring, and enormously rewarding enterprise. It needs to be done diligently, and decently, and on the basis of solid empirical evidence.

Note

1. American Economic Association, 2014 Broadway, Suite 305, Nashville, TN 37203; American Political Science Association, 1527 New Hampshire Avenue, NW, Washington DC 20036; American Psychological Association, 750 1st Street, NE, Washington DC 20002; American Sociological Association, 1527 New Hampshire Avenue, NW, Washington DC 20036.

References

Dorfman, J. *Thorsten Veblen and His America.* New York: Viking, 1934.

Feldman, K., and Newcomb, T. *The Impact of College on Students.* San Francisco: Jossey-Bass, 1969.

Geis, G., and Goff, C. "Introduction." In E. H. Sutherland, *White Collar Crime: The Uncut Version.* New Haven, Conn.: Yale University Press, 1983.

Gordon, V. *The Undecided College Student: An Academic and Career Advising Challenge.* Springfield, Ill.: Charles C. Thomas, 1984.

Havemann, E., and West, P. *They Went to College: The College Graduate in America Today.* New York: Harcourt, Brace, 1952.

Horowitz, I. L. *C. Wright Mills: An American Utopian.* New York: Free Press, 1983.

Marrow, A. J. *The Practical Theorist: The Life and Work of Kurt Lewin.* New York: Basic Books, 1979.

Mead, M. *Blackberry Winter: My Earlier Years.* New York: Morrow, 1972.

Newcomb, T., Koenig, K., Flacks R., and Warwick, D. *Persistence and Change: Bennington College and Its Students After 25 Years.* New York: Wiley, 1967.

Pascarella, E. T., and Terenzini, P. T. *How College Affects Students.* San Francisco: Jossey-Bass, 1991.

Riesman, D. "Law and Sociology: Notes on Recruitment, Training, and Colleagueship." *Stanford Law Review,* 1957, 643–673.

Riesman, D. "Foreword." In R. L. Weiss, *Loneliness*. Cambridge, Mass.: MIT Press, 1973, ix–xxii.

Skinner, B. F. *Particulars of My Life*. New York: Knopf, 1976.

GILBERT GEIS, sociologist and criminologist, is professor emeritus, the University of California, Irvine.

TED L. HUSTON is the Amy Johnson McLaughlin Centennial Professor of Human Ecology and professor of psychology at the University of Texas at Austin.

This chapter offers some general advice for faculty advisers but focuses on distinctive elements for advising in technical subjects, particularly in dealing with incoming transfer students who have technical credits to transfer. The chapter ends with a brief discussion of the use of computer-based information systems.

The Role of Faculty Advising in Science and Engineering

J. R. Cogdell

The oft-quoted remark[1] of President James Garfield about Mark Hopkins sitting on one end of a bench with Garfield on the other charms us because it pictures two important truths of education: (1) that basically education is communication between a faculty member and a student; and (2) the more intimate that communication, the more likely the results will be long lasting. This is true in the classroom, in the laboratory, and certainly in the faculty office, and it is true whether the communication is about English, calculus, or cell division. And it is doubly true when the subject is that mixture of personal, curricular, or professional matters we call academic advising.

Faculty are involved in advising students inevitably and in several modes. Faculty are periodically expected to review and approve the course selections of the students. At the other end of the spectrum, a few faculty naturally become surrogate fathers, mothers, and professional mentors for their students and clearly enjoy their constant friendship. This chapter is written for the faculty member who enjoys the routine advising of registration times and also wants to have more involvement with students in working through other advising questions. In other words, I am speaking to faculty who see academic advising as a major component of their contribution to their department and students. Normally, such faculty are rare and prized in words and should be increasingly rewarded with salary raises and promotions.

Academic advising assists the student in forming goals, in devising plans for accomplishing those goals, and in equipping the student to cope with any personal, intellectual, and institutional barriers that hinder the execution of that plan. In the following pages, I will speak briefly of advising by faculty generally, then address those unique aspects of advising in science and engineering. The evaluation of transfer students rates a separate section, and I conclude with a look at the future.

The Role of Faculty in Advising

Training. Training for advising is for the most part on-the-job as one sorts through the various sources of relevant information and develops contacts with more experienced advisers. Degree programs and institutional policies are defined in various places such as university and college catalogues, and in policy memoranda from deans and other officers. Many policies are unwritten, or at least not written in any obvious place. A way to master this constantly changing Byzantine body of knowledge is to adopt a "no goose chases" approach. When a student stumps me with a question, I do not send the student to someone else to find out the answer; rather, I get on the phone and call people who might know. Usually with persistence one can get an answer. In this way the adviser serves the student and also adds to his or her own knowledge.

Rules, Rules, Rules. Many rules and administrative procedures were formed to stop some abuse. For example, a rule in our college states that if a student is eligible to graduate during the next semester, he or she is *required* to graduate. This rule arose when we had many international students who were avoiding graduation because they did not want to return to their home countries, perhaps to face army service during an active war. But should this rule necessarily be applied blindly in any and all circumstances? Sometimes a student has legitimate educational reasons for delaying graduation (perhaps to take courses that are offered only once a year). I have been a successful advocate with the dean to permit such a student to remain in school for good cause. My point is that it isn't enough to know the rules; a good adviser should assess the extent to which the rule serves the best interests of the student and the institution in each specific instance.

Encouraging the Good Student. A reality is that 80 percent of the adviser's time is spent on 20 percent of the students, and these students represent the bottom 20 percent in academic standing. This is inevitably true because the students who are struggling academically need special care in selecting courses, in knowing what grades they must make to avoid expulsion, and in discussing alternatives in other disciplines or at other institutions. For this reason, it is easy to overlook the good student who makes steady progress toward graduation with strong grades. When I review the record of an excellent student, I try to acknowledge accomplishments and recognize the hard work required to achieve such a record. A simple "It is a pleasure to see such a good record. You must work very hard," will do. These students should be encouraged to attend graduate or professional schools. It is untrue that all high achievers are confident and self-motivated. We all need appreciation and encouragement.

Kindness to Off-Campus Visitors. Prospective students often travel great distances and thus deserve special consideration. Often these prospects have a long list of people and offices to visit and have limited time. As an adviser, I try to call ahead to make sure that the people they need to see are available. I also provide good directions, usually in the form of an annotated map, and I encourage them to call me if they have other questions after they leave campus. These simple courtesies not only allow the student to form a good first impression but are important recruitment.

Advising in Science and Engineering

Wrong Motives. Most students of science and engineering are preparing for a career after graduation. A problem arises when the student's choice is motivated by a high starting salary, ease of finding employment, or, worse still, his or her parents. I frequently ask students if they like to do homework; with this question I make the point that studies are likely to go well when grounded in intellectual engagement and vision for applying the acquired knowledge. Helping students explore their motives can save them time and money.

Highly Structured Curricula. Curricula in science and engineering are highly structured in two ways: (1) the student progresses from beginning to advanced courses; and (2) electives cluster around specific career paths. The hierarchical structure of knowledge leads to prerequisites, and specific career paths lead to preselected elective blocks of technical courses. A faculty adviser with knowledge of the technical subject and the profession is equipped to decide when the rules should be set aside in the student's best interest. Thus the adviser should spend some time understanding the student's ambitions, making recommendations that were unforeseen when the standard plans were devised.

Long-Range Planning. Many electives are offered once a year; a few are even offered only every other year. Students need to plan far into the future. The adviser can facilitate long-range planning by alerting the student and knowing when courses will be offered.

The Renaissance Adviser. Students in science and engineering, and faculty for that matter, tend to be narrow in their interests. This unfortunate cultural impoverishment can be countered to some degree by a faculty adviser who has read widely and who can bring broad experiences into the advising session. When I advise students, I try to look over their background records to identify some point of personal contact such as their hometown, other colleges, or job experiences that might lead to a pleasant conversation or even a learned discussion.

Don't Shoot from the Hip. How many times has a student stuck his or her head in the doorway and said, "Do you have time for a quick question?" For the student, it's a quick question involving an elective or a course substitution. When I look at the student's record, however, I often discover that the "quick question" involves many issues and requires careful analysis of the student's entire program. And any answer or agreement that comes out of the advising session should be recorded for future reference. For these reasons, I try to have the student's full records before me before I answer any question.

Advising of Transfer Students

The evaluation of incoming transfer credits is an important and exacting responsibility of the faculty adviser in science and engineering. We use a three-stage evaluation at the University of Texas at Austin. The admissions office evaluates the transcript and classifies routine courses such as English, chemistry, electives, and so on, to find equivalent courses. My office has asked the admissions department to honor hours of credit but not to grant course equivalencies for courses in the major. Then we interview the student to evaluate the major courses and to determine how the various incoming credits apply toward degree requirements. At this stage, we read course descriptions from college catalogues, and examine textbooks or at least the tables of contents to make sure that the appropriate topics were covered.

Since courses in the same subject are rarely identical at different colleges, and since prerequisite knowledge is essential to success in major courses, judgment must be used in dealing with these incoming credits. My goal is to give the students as much credit as possible, subject to protecting them from advancing to higher level courses without adequate background. Frankly, I would hate to make a student retake a course when he or she has covered 85 percent of the material already; occasionally, I will exempt the student, subject to his or her auditing informally a portion of a course to make up for missed material.

The third stage of the evaluation requires that the student demonstrate knowledge of the subject for which transfer credit is expected. I may sketch simple problems during the interview and ask the student to solve them. The idea is not so much to expect perfection as to engage in a technical conversation about the subject. If the student makes a good try and is able to understand the nature of their understanding or lack thereof, I am inclined to give credit. But if the student in effect refuses to work on the problem with excuses like, "It's been a year since I did that course," or "I can't remember the formula," then I suspect a weak background and am disinclined to grant transfer credit.

Transfer Students from International Institutions Over this decade, I have seen an increasing number of students transferring at junior and senior levels from international institutions to study undergraduate engineering. These students present special problems for evaluators. Especially in a small institution that accepts few international transfers, the admissions office may be unequipped to evaluate preparatory courses. Evaluators work from source books that caution giving too much credit for foreign programs, but often, in turn, evaluators may accept too little. Frequently I become the student's advocate with the admissions office to grant more credit for mathematics or science courses. For courses in the major, one has to look over the syllabus that the student brings, trying to sift the collegiate level work from the practical technology training frequently required in foreign programs.

Here, especially, the technical interview of the student is critical. On some occasions, I have delayed transfer credit for courses until I have examined the student's books for content and level. On more than one occasion, I have perused a book in Chinese on probability and random process theory, for example, and made a judgment based on the equations and figures. Of course, to make such a judgment, the adviser must know the technical content of the subject intimately. It may be necessary to refer students to other faculty who are more expert on the subject in question.

The quality and approaches of international institutions vary greatly, and I routinely ask the students to demonstrate knowledge of the subjects on their transcripts. This often shocks the students, who expected credit with no questions asked, so I allow them time to review the material before answering questions. In many instances the student has been allowed to delay a semester or more before returning to complete the evaluation.

Students with Technology and Military Training. Quite often, an incoming student has obtained a background in the practical dimensions of science and engineering through technology training or military school. This type of background is excellent motivation; it gives the student an appreciation of the educational opportunity they have. However, the preparation generally is not a substitute for college-level courses. Usually the students understand that they will receive little or no credit, but occasionally incoming students are quite upset that their background counts for nothing, as they see it. My policy is to permit such students to demonstrate knowledge on a final exam in the subject in question. I show them the book and syllabus and give them time to look over the materials. Usually the challenger will realize at this stage that practical knowledge will not carry him or her far enough to pass the exam. In other situations, we make arrangements for the student to take the final examination at the end of the semester with the rest of the students, to minimize additional work for the faculty.

The Older Student. Older students may come from industrial or military backgrounds; quite a few are seeking second degrees and second careers. These people generally are excellent students, but they often carry heavy workloads or family responsibilities and, as a result, make slower progress through the program. These people get a lot of sympathy and leeway from me, and I generally have to caution them about neglecting family and personal needs.

Future Trends

Resource Limitations. Colleges and universities are caught in a squeeze between diminishing resources and increasing demands for advising services. Inevitably, a greater number of professional advisers will be needed. In my department, we have recently eliminated one of the two faculty advisers, and the remaining one is assisted by two part-time staff advisers, as well as by paid and volunteer student advisers. This places the faculty adviser in the role of trainer, consultant, policy maker, and manager of advising services.

Information, Information. The adviser is a broker of information. After years of working through advising problems and exploring the information maze, one becomes something of a specialized sage. But how does one communicate all this information? Of course, we publish advising information sheets and student manuals, post notices on bulletin boards, and answer questions without end; but many students, and not a few faculty, still do not have the information they need to get through the various registrations, degree requirements, and so on.

New resources are becoming available. Computer networks, from the Internet to local departmental networks, are becoming common media for distributing such information. Gopher and Mosaic systems offer the possibility of maintaining a departmental database of advising information that can be available to every student who takes the trouble to log on and investigate. We have such a system under development, and some departments here at the University of Texas at Austin already have functioning systems.

Expert Systems. We also are developing computer-based advising systems. The registrar has created a program that performs degree audits to match student credits against degree requirements; the program also lists requirements that are unmet. This is a first step toward more active computer-based advising. We have under development a system that will go one step farther in that it will suggest courses for the coming semester based upon prerequisites and a critical path analysis toward graduation.

Person-to-Person. We end with the same image with which we began: the student on one end of a bench and the adviser on the other. Modern information technology cannot substitute for the relationship between student and adviser; indeed, the point is to free the advising session from routine information transfer and rules-quoting. Our hope is that our students will enjoy exploring cyberspace for information, but know when to come in for personal advising. We also are using the technology to search out students with special advising needs. Through the initiative of student or adviser, we hope to end up face to face on that bench.

Note

1. "Give me a log hut, with only a simple bench, Mark Hopkins at one end and I [sic] on the other, and you can have all the buildings, apparatus and libraries without him." Address to Williams College Alumni, New York, 1871. Hopkins was president of Williams College, 1836-1872.

J. R. COGDELL is associate professor and undergraduate adviser in the Department of Electrical and Computer Engineering at the University of Texas at Austin. Dr. Cogdell is author of Foundations of Electrical Engineering, *published by Prentice Hall.*

This chapter provides advice to faculty members just entering the
ranks of academic advisers. It offers some insights into common
perceptions and problems encountered in advising female students who
are pursuing majors in science and engineering.

Advising Women Considering Nontraditional Fields of Study

Leodocia M. Pope

One of the prominent themes of the nineties in academia is diversity—in course offerings and faculty experiences. This theme also is relevant to the changing demographics of today's colleges and universities. The composition of today's student body has been affected by career changes, the return of women to school, and development of an accessible community college system. Students today are entering disciplines which have been "off limits" largely for historic reasons; there is considerable effort expended to attract and track underrepresented groups such as women and ethnic minorities throughout their careers. Unfortunately, there is a high attrition rate for members of these groups at many points along their career paths. Increasing interest in the educational experience of these students is testimony to the growing recognition of the great need to attract and educate the most talented people regardless of their gender.

This chapter addresses the advising of women in academic disciplines in which they are underrepresented. The ways in which advisers can have an impact on the academic and professional careers of these students will be examined using both the experiences of women who have achieved successful and productive careers and also the perceptions and experiences of aspiring female scientists who are at the beginning of their professional lives. Much

The author is indebted to faculty members and students in the College of Engineering, Department of Chemistry, and the Department of Physics at the University of Texas at Austin for their time and willingness to share with me their past experiences and future expectations.

of the material for this chapter has been gathered through interviews with women in various career stages in science and engineering.

Women who enter disciplines in which they are historically underrepresented encounter many institutional and invisible barriers while developing their careers. To succeed in these disciplines and successfully navigate the academic course requires a very high level of persistence, motivation, and good coping skills. In a recent National Science Foundation (NSF) study (Ruskus and Williamson, 1993), the foremost barrier perceived by women pursuing a career in science or engineering is gender discrimination. Fully 41 percent of the participants polled in this study reported that they had experienced some form of gender discrimination. These data underline the importance of examining the insights of women in nontraditional disciplines such as science and engineering in order to learn how they have avoided the barriers perceived by so many other women in these areas.

It is common to enter into academic advising as part of one's "service to the department" duties. Faculty who enjoy interacting with students and who get pleasure from helping a student find the right career path often remain as student advisers in one capacity or another. Often, the names of these faculty members are spread via the student grapevine, and students will continue to seek them out even if they do not serve as official advisers. In my own case, it soon became apparent that advising students occurs in many different settings. It is important that departments offer a variety of settings that make it possible to reach out in ways that meet the different needs of students. Undergraduates need to make connections with faculty so that they can develop the skills necessary for the productive personal interactions that will be so important later on in professional life.

One-on-one is the most frequent advising scenario, most often occurring just prior to registration, with the student looking for someone to sign a course request form. This is probably the least satisfactory way of advising. There is often no attempt to discuss goals and expectations. Students may not ever see the same adviser. The faculty member "on duty" may see only a few random students and, therefore, feel as if time is being wasted. Another frequent advising experience is the just-before and just-after class encounter. These situations do serve a purpose in that students who are shy and lacking in self-confidence often find these interactions to be a major source of faculty guidance. Given the demands on time and other responsibilities, plus the lack of resources for advising, it is often difficult for even the most conscientious faculty members to respond to their students' needs on demand.

What is Advising?

Much of the advising process consists of a few questions and a signature. Fortunately, this situation is changing as many institutions are developing centers staffed with professional advisers who handle day-to-day questions dealing with degree requirements and other facets of student life not directly associated with the student's career development within an academic discipline. In the past, many institutions operated with a "weed-out" mentality, but many disciplines and academic departments are now beginning to focus on getting the right students and then working with them to make them successful. This presents faculty advisers with an important opportunity to help students to develop the skills necessary to make good decisions as their careers develop.

Why is Advising Different for Women in Nontraditional Disciplines?

Most female students respond to cues differently than do male students. Female students use language differently when describing their accomplishments and concerns (Conwell and Dresselhaus, 1994). Often, in nontraditional areas, faculty are not aware or experienced in interpreting and responding to the cues and language of their female students. Therefore, advisers must become particularly careful listeners in helping all students to become more aware of their potential. For example, since many of the women in the graduate engineering program at the University of Texas at Austin have entered from nonengineering backgrounds, these students especially need an adviser to help them learn to feel confident in a totally new culture. It is important for all departments, however, to provide support for female students to acquire the skills and self-assurance required for successful completion of their degrees and entry into graduate school and a productive professional life.

How Advisers Can Help Female Students Prepare for Graduate School or the Professional Work Place

There are a number of ways in which an adviser can help female students prepare for the competition of school and the work place.

Encourage activities that make it possible for students to find mentors and advisers. Many women scientists can credit one individual (the gender of this individual was of no consequence) whose support and encouragement at the undergraduate level was an important factor in their decision to attend graduate school. Providing facilities such as coffee rooms where faculty and students can gather is a productive method for encouraging the formation of supportive relationships between faculty and students. A room large enough to accommodate a table and chairs will encourage faculty and students to sit and talk for a few minutes each day in a "low-pressure" setting. In this way, students can connect with colleagues who may become mentors and collaborators. Female students may decide to leave programs during times of uncertainty and self-doubt. It is precisely this time when an adviser or mentor might make the difference. These sorts of interactions are important mechanisms for enhancing the self-confidence of female students who are inexperienced and feel isolated.

Help students understand the process into which they have entered. Many students are not aware of their progression along a pathway destined to help them function ultimately as independent scientists. Participation in activities that are designed to enhance self-confidence should be encouraged. These enable the student to learn to articulate her own career goals as well as to discuss pertinent scientific issues with peers. Recognizing that these opportunities are an important part of the educational process will be invaluable for helping students (especially women and minorities) to respond to this hidden agenda and to develop strategies necessary to achieve their full potential (Widnall, 1988).

Help students learn to network. Networking is an important skill for everyone to master, but it is critical for students who will ultimately be working in an isolating environment characteristic of many disciplines in natural science and engineering. It may be necessary to set up a working structure and then to let the student choose her own direction. Support groups can be organized so that students can meet each other and interact with professionals in their disciplines as well. Programs such as "Faculty Firesides" sponsored by the University of Texas Women in Engineering have been extremely successful because they provide a setting for developing networking skills between industrial contacts and students. These contacts then prove invaluable in future job searches.

Show that you are a human being. It is important for women students to realize that they do not have to be superhuman. Women students have lower career ambitions compared to their male cohorts (Widnall, 1988). Feelings of guilt about combining a career and family responsibilities make it critical that female students know how others in their chosen discipline have balanced career and family. They must recognize that all professional people with careers can and should have outside interests. Historically, many women with careers in science were forced by circumstance to make sacrifices such as not having a family or interests outside of their professions. Today, female students should be able to choose how much sacrifice is necessary in order to have a successful career in science.

Connect students with available campus resources when help is needed. Students experience tremendous stresses. Considerable numbers are forced to work in order to pay for their education. Many students are isolated from their families and peers. Many students who visit their advisers are really desperate for someone with whom to talk. It is important to recognize those students who are really asking you for help. Advising sometimes entails "fighting" for the student or connecting a student with the proper advocate. Become familiar with the resources available in your department and on campus; be prepared personally to connect your students with whatever services they might need. It is also important to know who the most helpful people are in the administrative offices. If a student feels comfortable enough with you to seek your aid, it is important that you take the initiative to connect him or her with the most effective person available. It is also important to follow up on your students.

Help students learn from the experiences of other women. It is very empowering to know what other women have done. How other women have managed their lives and what experiences and frustrations they have handled is useful information. Often faculty are uncomfortable revealing such personal information, for this type of sharing has the potential to create problems in the teacher-student relationship. Instead, there are excellent sources of professional histories of women in science (Gornick, 1983). Students should be encouraged to read this literature. A few useful references are listed at the end of this chapter. These histories are a combination of inspiring accounts of obstacles overcome as well as very sad chronicles of women who suffered because of overt and subtle discrimination by their colleagues and families. One can learn a great deal from the experiences of all of these women, and this information can be used to help devise a strategy for success.

Understand student language. Women are likely to assess their performance in courses differently than men. An experience commonly reported among women in nontraditional areas is that male peers were usually very positive in the assessment of their own performance in their courses, whereas women more often commented on some part of the course with which they were having difficulty. The common response by faculty and peers to these women's concerns was not "How can we help you to understand and apply this material?" but more often was "Well, perhaps you don't belong in this area." It is important to note that these reactions occurred with women who were at the top of their class and, in fact, were outperforming the very males who were so proud of their own performance.

Help students learn to diffuse stressful and uncomfortable situations. An important skill cited by many of the women interviewed was the ability to diffuse tense and unpleasant situations with humor. Some techniques can be acquired in a nonstressful setting. Encourage the formation of groups in which role playing can occur. These groups should be organized so that a minimum of effort by faculty is required for planning and implementation of the programs. Settings should be available where female students can acquire both the skills required for successful job interviews and the social interactions that are so necessary for professional advancement.

Advice to Advisers

These "nuggets" of advice have been acquired over the years and have proven invaluable in many advising situations.

1. Advisers cannot do everything themselves. It is important to identify colleagues/corporate contacts who will help. Names of individuals at various offices and agencies providing services to students in need are usually made available to all faculty members. Faculty members and administrators who are

willing to help students in emergency situations are a spin-off of your own networking skills. Get to know those who are student oriented.

2. You must be a good listener. Listen to whatever is important to the student who has sought you out, whether the issue is about academic concerns or personal problems. Students who are under a great deal of stress often just want to talk to someone. By listening, you perform an enormous service to them. Be aware that even though some women frequently visit with the adviser to discuss a seemingly trivial matter, these students really just want to connect on a personal level. The adviser must be prepared to take some time and have a private setting for these visits.

3. Be poised to recognize students who need encouragement and positive support. Several authors argue that exposure to an environment that neither encourages nor discourages but rather leaves the individual alone to cope can, in fact, be very discouraging to females (Betz, 1989 and Freeman, 1979). The ultimate effect of this environment on the students is to limit the full use and development of their abilities.

Although advising produces few tangible rewards for faculty, it can be an extremely satisfying endeavor. There can be no more important achievement than to help a young woman to articulate her dream. You should derive pleasure from the differences you make in the lives of your students. Count each student that you have "groomed" for science as an achievement. It is important to remember that the real continuity of science depends on those teachers and advisers who will identify and inspire a new generation of scientists.

Conclusion: What Can Advisers Learn from Successful Women?

Allowing for individual differences, many women who have achieved success in nontraditional disciplines share a number of the following characteristics. Their parents and/or teachers had high expectations and many were influenced by a significant teacher mentor. On the whole, they are realistic in assessments of people and situations, are not afraid of risk, and possess a generally positive outlook. They do not waste time, but stay focused on the long-term goal without being distracted from the job at hand. They are able to establish a mutually beneficial situation with spouse or partner.

Upon recognizing any of these characteristics, the faculty adviser can do much to encourage their development. Actively thinking about these factors can form the basis for positive interactions with students who seek your counsel. A number of the women interviewed for this chapter recounted how their careers were influenced by random events. At these turning points, adviser intervention is often the key element in career opportunities. Thus, it is important to be alert and to recognize situations that will open doors for your students.

References

Betz, N. E. "Implications of the Null Environment Hypothesis for Women's Career Development and for Counseling Psychology." *Counseling Psychologist,* 1989, *17* (1), pp. 136–144.

Conwell, E. M., and Dresselhaus, M. S. (eds.). *Women Scientists and Engineers Employed in Industry. Why So Few?* Washington, D.C.: National Academy Press, 1994.

Freeman, J. "How to Discriminate Against Women Without Really Trying." In J. Freeman (ed.), *Women: A Feminist Perspective.* (2nd ed.) Palo Alto, Calif.: Mayfield, 1979.

Gornick, Vivian. *Women in Science: Portraits from a World in Transition.* New York: Simon and Schuster, 1983.

Ruskus, J., and Williamson, C. *The Visiting Professorships for Women Program: Lowering the Hurdles for Women in Science and Engineering: Final Report* (NSF 93-159). Menlo Park, Calif.: SRI International, 1993.

Widnall. S. "AAAS Presidential Lecture: Voices from the Pipeline." *Science,* 1988, *241,* 1740–1745.

Additional Resources

Benditt, J. (ed.). "Women in Science, 1st Annual Survey." *Science,* 1992, *255,* pp. 1365–1388.

In this series of articles look for the following:

Amato, I., "Profile of a Field: Women Have Extra Hoops to Jump Through," pp. 1372–1373.

Gibbons, A., "Key Issue: Mentoring." pp. 1368–1369.

Gibbons, A. "Key Issue: Two-Career Science Marriage." pp. 1380–1381.

Selvin, P. "Profile of a Field: Heroism is Still the Norm." pp. 1382–1383.

Freeman, J. "How to Discriminate Against Women Without Really Trying." In J. Freeman (ed.), *Women: A Feminist Perspective.* (2nd ed.) Palo Alto, Calif.: Mayfield, 1979.

Gornick, V. *Women in Science: Portraits from a World in Transition.* New York: Simon and Schuster, 1983.

Widnall, S. "AAAS Presidential Lecture: Voices from the Pipeline." *Science,* 1988, *241,* pp. 1740–1745.

LEODOCIA M. POPE is senior lecturer in the Department of Microbiology at the University of Texas at Austin. She has been involved in advising students in natural sciences and has served as faculty sponsor for the undergraduate organization for students in microbiology and medical technology.

Prospective faculty mentors often ask, "What does mentoring involve?"
This chapter considers that question from an experiential point of view.

Faculty as Mentors

Jeanne M. Lagowski, James W. Vick

Mentor and *mentoring* are frequent words in the academic environment. These words can also be the source of considerable misunderstanding. Students' expectations of a mentor can—and often do—differ widely from faculty perceptions of what being a mentor involves. This gap may arise in part because the word *mentor* has several quite different accepted meanings: adviser, counselor, guide, preparer, monitor, teacher, instructor, professor, coach, preceptor, proctor, master, friend, and guru (Roget, 1977; Random House, 1984; Funk and Wagnalls, 1963). Faculty who think of mentoring almost exclusively in terms of imparting knowledge in their discipline will probably not be effective mentors for students who expect advice, counsel, and guidance from a faculty member who is also a friend.

Even though mentoring may mean different things to different people, we firmly believe that faculty can be highly effective mentors. The requirements are minimal, but essential: a sincere interest in students as individuals, an open mind, flexibility, and a willingness to assume roles that extend beyond traditional classroom activities. The rewards are many. Opportunities to make a difference abound.

There is no single job description for mentors. Aside from the dictates of common courtesies and professional behavior, there are no rules either. There is no right or wrong way to serve as a mentor. It will be different—indeed must be different—for different students. Mentoring relationships are unique to the people involved. Mentoring is also dynamic; it changes and evolves as the student matures and as he or she needs change. By contrast, faculty who are regarded by students as effective mentors have some common characteristics.

The poem quoted in this chapter is from *It's Always Too Soon to Quit*, by Lewis R. Timberlake. Copyright 1988. Used by permission of Fleming H. Revell, a division of Baker Book House.

79

In this chapter, we propose to share some experiences and impressions gained through our work as faculty members and providers of student services.

Although there are no rules for mentors, there are some things that almost go without saying. The student must be accepted as an individual who has been shaped and influenced by many different forces and experiences and who holds personal opinions and beliefs. Mentors must be nonjudgmental and open-minded. Good communication based on openness and mutual trust is essential.

The goal—and the challenge—of mentoring is to help make the student's educational experience more personally rewarding. It is a *supportive process*. It is a process "in which a more skilled or more experienced person, serving as a role model, nurtures, befriends, teaches, sponsors, encourages, and counsels a less skilled or less experienced person for the purpose of promoting the latter's professional and/or personal development" (Anderson and Shannon, 1988). Ideally, mentoring is a *long-term* commitment. The most productive relationship would begin early in a student's college years and extend to, and perhaps beyond, graduation.

Compatibility of mentor and student is basic to the success of any mentoring relationship. Pairing by assignment based on presumed fit or perceived commonality of interests does not guarantee success. Many of the most successful relationships seem to grow out of a mutual adoption process. For example, during the course of a semester a student and teacher may gradually establish a relationship involving interest and respect that extends well beyond the last day of the course. Conversations that initially focused on course-related material gradually extend to include hints on how to study more effectively. Mentors provide words of encouragement and advice, and discussion of the student's interests and goals. To be effective, both parties must want to be involved in the mentoring relationship. If either party does not want to be involved, the relationship will not work. Mentoring cannot be legislated or forced.

Availability and *approachability* are clearly keys to successful mentoring. If students do not feel welcome and comfortable talking with you, they will simply not take advantage of opportunities for one-to-one interactions or follow through on invitations, no matter how sincerely intended. Similarly, it is difficult to restrict interactions, such as during narrowly defined office hours. Within reason, mentors need to be available when the student seeks their guidance, support, or encouragement.

Make the students feel welcome. Invite them to your office. When they come, give them your full attention. Show that you are interested in them by asking open-ended questions about them. Get them to talk. Be a good listener. Encourage them to come back again and give them an idea of what times are good for you. Exchange phone numbers and/or e-mail addresses. Make a notation on your calendar so that you initiate the next visit if you have not heard from the student.

Faculty mentors are in a unique position to *provide realistic encouragement* to students. The key word here is "realistic." Honesty is absolutely essential, though the adviser must not be cruel or hurtful. This is sometimes difficult; it requires sensitivity and careful word choice. Although telling students what they want to hear may be momentarily less painful for both parties, it is not a favor to either.

By virtue of their expertise and experience, faculty are also in a unique position to help students assess the reality of successfully pursuing a major and ultimately a career in their disciplines. Consider, for example, a student who expresses great interest in the field, but who earns a C in a basic core course. Should this student be encouraged to pursue more advanced study in the discipline based upon apparent talent that is not reflected in the grade? Or, was that C earned by tenaciously "gutting out" the course? What about the student who was inspired and excited by an experience in one course, but who begins to have second thoughts because the next course turns out to be dull or difficult? Faculty mentors can help students realistically evaluate their interests in the light of their abilities and can help them to differentiate between experiences that are substantive and those that are not.

Everyone enjoys a sincere compliment, and a few simple words of encouragement from a respected mentor sometimes have far-reaching impact. For example, some science majors who ultimately became science writers were strongly influenced by a teacher or mentor who told them that they seemed to have a way with words and an ability to express complex ideas clearly and succinctly.

Encouragement can often be given by simply communicating faith in a student's ability. Some students overtly seek this kind of encouragement; for example, a student may pop into your office on the morning of a big exam and say, "Wish me luck!" Others respond to a challenge such as the bet of a soft drink that they will attain some goal, for example a B on a particular exam or in a particular course. If you know the student, it is easy to couch the terms of the bet so that the student will look forward to collecting after a win but can easily ignore or forget to pay off following a loss. If the student appears and you go together to the Student Union to settle the bet, the conversation will almost certainly start with the student's analysis of the success (or lack of success) in achieving the grade, and will develop into an open discussion of topics such as self-perceptions or dealing with disappointment, subjects that are often difficult to discuss otherwise.

Faculty mentors are important and valuable sounding boards as students make decisions concerning electives or career paths. What courses are particularly important in building a solid knowledge base? What are good buttressing courses to broaden and to complement that knowledge base? Should internships, study abroad, volunteer work, or job experience be part of the plan? Is graduate or professional school training required? If graduate work is required, where should students apply to undertake this work, given their interests, abilities, and competitiveness?

Effective mentoring involves *knowing the campus resources available and making effective referrals.* Faculty members' expertise is in their academic disciplines and the pedagogical aspects of transferring knowledge to their students. They are usually not experts in learning and test-taking skills, career counseling, psychological counseling, or financial aid. However, other members of the campus community can provide this help. Some campuses also have professional staff counselors and advisers who are highly knowledgeable about degree requirements, university regulations, and other aspects of academic advising for which faculty typically are the least comfortable. Faculty mentors should freely refer students who could benefit from these colleagues' professional expertise, but they should do so in a way that both encourages the student to follow through and that leads to a positive experience. This is especially important when the mentor has information, often gleaned over a period of time or at an emotional cost to the student, that would facilitate the next interaction and make it less stressful for the student. A telephone call, a simple handwritten note carried by the student or, in more complex cases, a note that invites a return call so that you can provide background information can make the difference between a good experience and one that is less satisfactory.

An important corollary of knowing the resources available is to *know your own limitations*. No one can be an expert in everything, and students do not expect you to be. It is not a kindness to provide advice and counsel that is inaccurate or out of date. In fact, such advice can be very costly. For example, taking the wrong course or taking a course for which the student does not have the prerequisites can easily cost an extra semester.

Knowing both your own limitations *and* the campus resources available is especially critical should you find yourself faced with a student in crisis. Fortunately these situations do not occur very often, but when they do, it is necessary to remain calm and to communicate your concern to the student, while simultaneously arranging for someone with the appropriate professional expertise to help him or her. In some cases, it is important not only to make the initial referral contact, but to accompany the student personally and stay with him or her until someone else takes over, for example, if the student appears suicidal. Don't take chances! Other situations are not the same kinds of emergencies, but are crises nonetheless: for example, cases involving rape and substance abuse. Professional help is available in the psychological counseling center or at the student health center, and it is always a good idea to keep their phone numbers readily available. If you happen to know or have worked with anyone in those offices, keep their name(s) on file too; these people can be helpful in arranging a prompt referral. To be sought out by students in a time of crisis speaks to their trust in you and is perhaps one of the most sincere compliments that a mentor can receive.

Another important role of the faculty mentor involves *helping students become more marketable and learning how to market themselves*. Development of good communication skills, both written and oral, takes time, and the students who most need to work on these skills are often the very ones who try to delay taking that composition course because they fear they will not do well in it. The possibility of taking a speech course as an elective probably never crossed their minds. The importance of neatly and carefully prepared applications and resumés cannot be overstressed. Prospective graduate and professional school students frequently underestimate the amount of time it takes to prepare their applications. Are there extracurricular activities that would help develop important skills, such as leadership, or that would test the student's commitment to working in a helping profession? The faculty mentor is the ideal person to talk about these things in generalities, but there is probably a wealth of campus resources that can be tapped once students realize the importance of working on their writing skills, developing a good resumé, going through a mock interview, or doing volunteer work.

Faculty mentors should be able to serve as a knowledgeable reference. Applications for a scholarship, a job, or admission to graduate or professional school invariably require recommendations or letters of evaluation. Potential employers, selection committees, and admissions committees often use these letters to decide whether or not to interview an applicant or to choose among applicants with similar credentials. A thoughtful, well-written letter that is tailored for the intended purpose, portrays the student as a three-dimensional human being, and speaks to personal qualities that are germane can make a tremendous difference in how the student's application is handled. Sadly, on many campuses today, especially the larger ones, many students feel that no one knows them well enough to write such a letter. All too many students are disadvantaged by so-called recommendations that add nothing to what could be readily gleaned from their transcripts. In the students' eyes, knowing them well enough to provide a "good [insightful] recommendation," and doing so in a timely manner, is one of the most important roles of a faculty mentor.

Since faculty mentors know the students with whom they work well, they are in an ideal position to *encourage students to apply for, or to nominate them for, various awards, scholarships, and other forms of recognition* including the more select positions that are open to students on the campus, such as student ombudsman. Some students are very assertive in this realm, but others who could be strong candidates are unaware of such opportunities or are hesitant to come forward on their own. They underestimate their own competitiveness. Not every student will be a viable candidate, of course, but many have been pleasantly surprised at what is possible if they make the effort and take the chance. Many an encouraging mentor has received some version of a note that says, "Thanks for all you've done for me. I got the scholarship!"

A good mentor is a *role model.* In a sense, students see faculty as standards, as people who have achieved a certain professional stature. Consciously or unconsciously, they compare and contrast themselves as they evaluate their progress and refine their goals. This is particularly true of their faculty mentor because they know that person better than they do most of their teachers.

Decision making is the student's responsibility. The mentor is the ideal person to help a student identify and discuss options. Who is in a better position to help reflect on the pros and cons of the various options? To counsel and advise as the student tries to make choices? The line can become very fine, but the mentor should remain neutral and leave the decisions to the student.

Failure is never final! One of the more difficult roles of a mentor is to help students deal with failure. Failure in the academic world comes in many guises, ranging from one disappointing examination, to dealing with a frustrating relationship, to not getting the job or being accepted to the graduate or professional school of choice. The following lines from a poem in a book by Lewis Timberlake (1988, p. 58) seem particularly appropriate.

> Failing doesn't mean I'm a failure;
> it just means I haven't yet succeeded.
> Failing doesn't mean I have accomplished nothing;
> it just means I've learned something . . .
> Failing doesn't mean I've been disgraced;
> it just means I dared to try.
> Failing doesn't mean I don't have what it takes;
> it just means I must do things differently next time.
> Failing doesn't mean I'm inferior;
> it just means I'm not perfect.
> Failing doesn't mean I've wasted my time;
> it just means I have reason to start over.
> Failing doesn't mean I should give up;
> it just means I must try harder.
> Failing doesn't mean I'll never make it;
> it just means I need more patience.
> Failing doesn't mean I'm wrong;
> it just means I must find a better way.

This poem was attached to a note from a recent graduate that read, "I had to send you this poem because it reminded me of our conversations last year. Thank you for being there when I so desperately needed someone who *believed in me.*"

Failure is an important aspect of learning, of defining one's strengths and weaknesses, one's likes and dislikes. The student who never tries and never runs the risk of failure will never know his or her capabilities. An understanding, insightful mentor can often help the student avoid unwise risks without eliminating potential opportunities for personal and intellectual growth.

For those who may want to pursue the topic of faculty mentoring further, a paper by Selke and Wong (1993), which discusses mentoring-empowered graduate advising, provides a good entry point into the literature.

As indicated at the beginning of this chapter, there is no one, right way to serve as a mentor for students. Any approach that falls within the bounds of professional behavior and that allows you to interact comfortably and effectively with the student in question is acceptable. To quote one of our colleagues who has been a particularly effective mentor, "When students come to me, I always try to treat them as I would want one of my own children treated." This paraphrasing of the Golden Rule could certainly serve as the motto for all faculty mentors.

References

Anderson, E., and Shallon, A. "Toward a Conceptualization of Mentoring." *Journal of Teacher Education*, 1988, *39*(1), pp. 38–42.

Funk and Wagnalls, *New Standard Dictionary of the English Language*, New York, 1963.

Roget's International Thesaurus, 4th Edition. New York: Harper & Row, 1977.

The Random House Thesaurus, College Edn., New York: Random House.

Selke, M.J., and Wong, T.D. "The Mentoring-Empowered Model: Professional Role Functions in Graduate Student Advisement." *NACADA Journal*, 1993, *13*(2), pp. 21–26.

Timberlake, Lewis R. *It's Always Too Soon to Quit*. Grand Rapids, Mich.: Fleming H. Revell, 1988.

JEANNE M. LAGOWSKI and JAMES W. VICK are both at The University of Texas at Austin. Lagowski is associate dean for health professions in the College of Natural Sciences and professor of zoology. Vick is vice president for student affairs and professor of mathematics.

*This chapter provides an overview of how faculty members may use
assessment evidence to understand students, evaluate the advising
process, and document the educational outcomes of advising.*

Academic Advising and Assessment

Gary R. Hanson, Christine Huston

Fall semester starts next week and there are a dozen students waiting outside my door. I desperately need to finish my syllabus, and as I unlock the
office door, the phone is ringing. I ask the first student to wait until I answer
the phone. Wouldn't you know? The department chair wants to talk about
academic advising. Doesn't she know there is a line outside my door? Her
request, one I've heard before, is to set up a meeting to talk about using
assessment information in our academic advising efforts. She wants *all* of
the faculty to participate this time, and wants me to come with some new
ideas. I listen to myself saying, "Yes, I'll come and try and give that some
thought ahead of time." I wonder when I'll find time to fit another meeting
into my chaotic schedule. As I motion for the first student to come in, I
think to myself that assessment and academic advising certainly seem to be
strange partners. That thought dies a quick and silent death when John
comes in asking me whether I think he should take algebra or calculus during his first semester as a freshman. How could assessment ever help me
with academic advising?

If that scenario sounds familiar, you are in good company. Nearly everyone involved in academic advising has too many responsibilities and too little
time to complete them. Adding assessment to academic advising often is
greeted with very little enthusiasm. Who needs assessment and why should
we care? The answer is: All of us need and use assessment everyday *because* we
care. We may not be aware of, nor do we always appreciate the vital role of
assessment, but it is there. Knowing what it is and how to use it can and will
improve your academic advising.

The purpose of this chapter is to illustrate how you can use assessment to
facilitate your advising efforts. We will discuss what assessment is and what it

is not. We will identify three broad categories of assessment used in academic advising and present a few examples of how we have used assessment information in our advising efforts.

What Is Assessment?

Assessment is all about being curious, about asking questions, and about finding and sharing answers—something most of us do every day. We may not call it assessment, but we infuse our lives with it. Assessment is merely a quest to answer our frustrations and dilemmas about advising. As with all adventures, there is neither a starting nor an ending point. Assessment is like peeling an infinite onion. You will need to peel many layers. With each layer, you learn something new and discover how very much more there is to learn, if only you could just get to the next layer. Much like cooking with onions, using assessment in academic advising can add a great deal of flavor to your life and can bring more than a few tears to your eyes.

Assessment involves asking questions. We can start by presenting a few questions about advising as illustrations of how we pursued them to their conclusions and, more importantly, how we used the answers we found to improve our academic advising. We believe there are three basic, but complex, questions advisers need to ask themselves. The first question is as follows: "Who uses academic advising and why?" We might ask why all those students are standing in a line outside the professor's office door on Monday morning the day before classes begin. On a more personal level, we may ask why John, who seems well prepared, is hesitant to take a calculus course.

The second question addresses another point: "How do students experience their academic advising?" What is the advising process like on your campus? Do students have one adviser throughout their academic career? How many different people do students consult to meet their advising needs? When should students be advised? When do they seek help? All of these questions deal with how students interact with their advisers. We can use assessment information to make advising more effective for the student and the adviser while improving and streamlining its delivery.

The third area deals with the effectiveness of academic advising. "Am I doing a good job as an adviser?" and "How do students benefit from the advising they receive?" are questions to ask. There are a number of ways to address these questions. How satisfied are students after talking with me? Are my students taking an appropriate level and sequence of courses? How well do they perform academically? Do the students who need to change majors find appropriate alternatives? Are students graduating from my institution in a reasonable period of time? Are they entering jobs in occupations related to their educational programs? Gathering and using assessment information to answer these questions will help you and your colleagues evaluate your effectiveness.

These three basic questions form the foundation of a good assessment plan. Such a plan involves systematically collecting, analyzing, and sharing information about advisees, the advising process, and the important educational outcomes that result from advising efforts. Within these three questions, assessment information may be obtained at multiple levels: (1) at the personal level of the student and/or the adviser, (2) at the department or college level, and (3) at the campus-wide level. In the discussion that follows, we provide examples at each level. Also, note that multiple methods may be used to collect the assessment data. Sources of information like personal interviews, clinical impressions, and focus group discussions are just as important as standardized tests, surveys, and academic transcript information.

Who Uses Academic Advising and Why?

The same kinds of data can be used to understand students at (1) the individual or personal level, and at (2) the group or aggregate level. For example, results from a mathematics placement test may be used to help John understand his readiness for calculus. A report of the ranges of the placement test scores ranges for all mathematics majors, sent to the head of the math department, would serve quite a different purpose. Such information might be used, for example, to track success of students in the program as a function of placement test scores. Both uses require an understanding of the meaning of the placement examination results. To describe the kinds of assessment information academic advisers may find useful in understanding students at the individual or personal level, we have included a brief example that describes working with one student. Following that example, we will present a brief example of how we use aggregate data about many students to help individuals make important academic and career decisions.

Using assessment data at the personal level means finding information that is personally relevant and useful to the student. For example, John's adviser needs to get to know him as an individual in order to provide useful advice. In addition to knowing John's standardized test scores and past academic performance, the adviser needs to learn something about the student's educational and career goals, hobbies, interests, and expectations about college. To help him make sound decisions, the adviser needs to know where John is coming from and where he wants to go.

If one regards advising as a form of teaching, advisers should be as well prepared for an advising appointment as they are to teach a class. Ideally, being prepared means gathering information about the student before the first advising appointment and then keeping notes on the discussion. Advising becomes a more rewarding and interesting job when you know something about the student's background and can track the student's development through a record of your discussions. Some faculty may feel uncomfortable with the notion of gathering personal information. But the information that is helpful is not of a deeply personal nature. If it is gathered with genuine interest in the well-being of the student, few students would consider it overly intrusive. Many institutions and advising units ask first-year students to complete a questionnaire designed by the unit which provides relevant information about the student's personal background and educational plans. In addition, many institutions use the self-reported information provided by students when they register to take the SAT or ACT.

John's apparently simple question, "Should I take algebra or calculus?" brings up a counter set of questions on the part of an astute adviser. The adviser first checks John's preparation for calculus. What was his score on the math achievement test? What math courses did he complete in high school? What were his grades? The adviser might even check to see if John took math in his senior year; this will reveal if John's math skills might be a little rusty.

An adviser gains valuable insight by knowing something about a student's family background. Awareness of the educational level of family members, where the parents and older siblings went to college, the occupations of family members, and whether a language other than English is spoken at home provides valuable insight. In response to John's question of whether he should take algebra or calculus during his first semester in college, the adviser could simply check whether he scored high enough on his math placement test to take calculus and leave it at that. On the other hand, knowing that John's mother has an MBA and that his father is an engineer, and seeing John's reluctance about taking calculus, an observant adviser might want to ask John about the source of his anxiety. If the student is feeling a great deal of pressure from his parents to begin at an advanced level, as the adviser suspects, the adviser could help the student realistically assess for himself the appropriate math level. Helping John articulate his parents' and his own concerns may help him subsequently to discuss his decision with them.

More than three quarters of all undergraduates express uncertainty about their choice of major. At the University of Texas at Austin, more than 80 percent of the students change majors at least once. Freshmen enter college with little information about either majors or careers. Knowing the range of majors John has considered and the reasons for considering them can stimulate a more productive discussion of whether his present major is a good fit. It is possible that John's reluctance to take calculus is a reflection of his uncertainty about his choice of a major. John may have chosen pre-med biology as a major because his family thinks he is strong in natural sciences and they want him to be a doctor. John, on the other hand, loves to write and always dreamed of being a journalist. His reluctance to take calculus may be related to the fact that he is also taking physics, chemistry, and biology. He may feel that by taking all math and science courses, he is getting in over his head and eliminating the opportunity to explore journalism while he pursues pre-med. Further discussion may uncover his desire to substitute a writing course. Ultimately, the question of whether to take algebra or calculus may turn on how sure he is about his choice of a major.

Establishing quick rapport with an advisee is enhanced by knowing something about the student's extracurricular activities and hobbies in high school as well as those planned for college. Being able to say, "I see you were a varsity volleyball player in high school" quickly communicates to the student that you have taken the trouble to learn something about her, and that she is not "just a number" after all. The same information can give you clues to a possible majors, choices of elective courses, reading experience, and a general sense of the student's goals. In John's case, the fact that he edited the student newspaper, read an astounding number of books in his senior year of high school, and won a short story contest are important facts to discuss with John, particularly if his confusion about his choice of a major develops. Further, knowing that a student plans to join clubs and social organizations, march in the school band, and work twenty hours a week would be important background information when discussing the challenges of getting admitted to medical school.

Being aware of students' expectations and concerns about college—the reasons they are attending, the grade point average they hope to make, the number of hours they intend to study, and their perception of their own study skills—can help an adviser assess how realistically the students are viewing the college curriculum. This type of information can alert an adviser to potential problems before the student encounters academic difficulty.

Data compiled in this manner can paint a portrait of an individual student. We use an instrument called the Educational Planning Survey to collect and summarize these kinds of assessment data about an individual student. The same pigments and elements—information about student's interests, aptitudes, background, and goals—when placed on the canvas side-by-side inevitably produce an image that can provide focus and insight when working with an individual student. The adviser who has not gathered, or bothered to assimilate, the kind of information necessary to conjure up a clear portrait of the advisee operates at a considerable disadvantage.

We can further understand each student within the context of other students' portraits. Many campuses use normative information such as SAT or ACT scores, or develop their own tests to help students in the advising process. For example, on the authors' campus, an individualized academic profile is given to students during the summer orientation program. The first section of the profile uses SAT Verbal and Math scores that compare the individual's results with those of other students. This information, when coupled with supportive academic advising, can help students understand the university's academic climate and their own relative strengths and weaknesses in broad academic areas. The course placement section of the profile provides information about whether students have met course prerequisites and how well they might expect to do in specific courses. A prediction of the student's success is calculated on the basis of a formula that compares his or her high school rank and test scores to those students who have just taken the course. A recommendation is printed on the profile. The recommendation in the context of the advising interview helps students make informed decisions on whether to take key courses or take preparatory courses first. The last section of the profile shows the distribution of first-year grades earned by freshmen with test scores and high school percentile ranks similar to those of the student. The grade distribution always ranges from very high to very low and illustrates vividly that academic success is within the student's control. When students are aware of discrepancies between their academic goals and their level of preparation, they are empowered to make informed choices and perhaps to avoid potential problems.

Assessment tools are more powerful when they are used in concert with one another. A student's score on the verbal section of the SAT has meaning only by virtue of its comparison with other scores. Multi-dimensional portraits of students contain information about both the individual elements and their configuration. A low SAT verbal score, when coupled with a low math score, creates a different image than when such a score is coupled with a high math score. The SAT scores take on an even different meaning when coupled with information that the student wants to be a biology major, speaks English as a second language, and that the student is a first-generation college student enrolled at an institution populated by students whose parents, and even grandparents, typically have a college education.

How Does Academic Advising Work?

When we ask questions about the academic advising process, we need to collect assessment information about whom students see, how often they seek advising, and what they discuss with their advisers. The specific questions to ask are shaped by the "model" of academic advising used on your campus. At our campus, we have many different models for delivering advising. For the purposes of this chapter, we will focus on how the academic advising process works for faculty. Understanding when students seek advising, what issues they find most important, how many different advisers they see, and how many times during the semester they seek help are important kinds of assessment information. If you routinely collect these data and use them to understand your advising delivery system and student advising experience, you can be more effective.

In this section, we want to share an example of how we collected information about the advising process on our campus. We used three types of assessment information to understand our academic advising process. We collected assessment information using student focus groups, a traditional paper and pencil survey, and several open-ended questions. Each type of assessment information provided a slightly different perspective that we used to develop a composite picture of the effectiveness of our advising system.

By sharing a brief summary of our results, we hope you will see the value in what we learned about advising on our campus. What did we find? First, we learned that many students (30 percent, or nearly 10,000 students on our campus) did not obtain any academic advising at all. Seventy-five percent of the students who talked to any adviser sought the counsel of multiple advisers during any given semester. One-stop shopping was *not* the norm! In addition, the advising process for most students on our campus appeared to be a series of short bursts of activity. Most students met with an adviser about four times during the semester, but rarely did the advising sessions last more than fifteen minutes.

What did students talk about during their advising session? The most frequently cited topic was the mechanics of course selection and registration and how to meet graduation requirements. Students were least likely to talk about personal problems, tutoring, life after college, and study techniques. When we asked students whether the advising process they experienced met their advising needs, more than 75 percent agreed. When we asked how satisfied they were with the help they received regarding specific topics, less than 50 percent of the students said they were satisfied with any particular advising topic. However, most were neutral or noncommittal; very few expressed dissatisfaction. We also used the open-ended comments and the focus group assessment information to evaluate the advising process. Several themes emerged from these data. We learned that many of our students had very positive experiences. They said things like, "My adviser was very thoughtful and considerate," or "My advisers have been exceptionally helpful and I felt they genuinely cared about me and my well-being." We also received negative comments. Some students perceived our advising process as impersonal, that too many advisers communicated inaccurate or incomplete information, and that advising should involve more than formal approval for course selection and registration. One commented, "Advisers are seemingly roped into advising students during registration, and they hurry them in and out." Another added, "They are unconcerned and uninformed." A third concluded, "The long lines combined with the patronizing attitude of advisers makes it a very unpleasant experience."

We also use another assessment method to help answer how students use our advising services. We collect and monitor information about student "flow" through the Undergraduate Advising Center, a centralized advising office used by undeclared majors. A similar tracking system could be implemented for a faculty-based advising system. Every time a student schedules an appointment with an academic adviser, assessment information is entered into a computerized tracking system. The date, the adviser visited, the nature of the visit (e.g., course selection, personal issues, career counseling) and the student identification are collected at the time the student talks with the adviser. The information is entered on a daily basis and the tracking system allows office staff to select various summary statistical reports at any given point in time. Some reports provide summary statistics by adviser to indicate the number of students advised while others summarize the frequency of issues discussed during the advising sessions for particular advisers or the office as a whole. Other reports summarize the "flow" of students through the office by week. At the end of each semester, a complete history can be generated by selecting various reports from a menu on the computer terminal. The information provides important indicators of the workload and the nature of the problems students encounter during each week of the semester. This information allows the advisers to plan their workload, to understand the nature of what they may expect from students in the future as well as to maintain contact with students who have not requested help but may be doing poorly in some of their classes. This tracking system would also assist faculty to negotiate a balance between their teaching and advising responsibilities.

Both of these examples show how helpful it is to monitor the process of academic advising. Without assessment, it is difficult to determine whether the delivery of advising is working and when, where, and how to change the process to serve students more successfully. Such assessment information makes it possible to accurately focus efforts to improve the advising system.

How Do We Know If Our Advising Is Effective?

Your students' academic success is one of the gauges by which you can measure your success as an adviser. For one individual, success may mean earning a 3.8 grade point average (GPA) and working on a professor's research project as a way to prepare for graduate school. For another student, success may mean making slow but steady progress toward a degree and clinging to a 2.3 GPA while working thirty hours a week and supporting a family. For large groups of students, the effectiveness of advising can be gauged by comparing their average cumulative GPAs to those of similar groups of students who have had different advising experiences. If students are assisted in selecting courses and ultimately choose majors that fit their level of preparation, abilities, and interests, they are more likely to make reasonable progress toward a degree without ending up in academic difficulty.

Just as student evaluations can help you improve your teaching, they can help you assess and strengthen your advising skills. Academic advisers perform at least two roles: They provide information and serve as counselors. To address these two roles, you might use a systematic survey of students to ask if the adviser is approachable, is a good listener, and is genuinely concerned about students. Questions could also ask students about how knowledgeable the adviser is about career options, appropriate referrals, degree requirements, and courses that complement their interests. In addition to getting general feedback related to the essential roles of an adviser, one can customize a survey to gain insight regarding some special concern of the adviser or department.

Student outcomes and survey data can be used together to evaluate an advising program and contribute to its improvement. We would like to describe an evaluation process that could be used at any institution. The process was used to determine the effect of a new summer advising program set up to help freshmen with undeclared majors work with advisers to begin to think about the process of selecting a major and to select courses suitable to their goals and academic background.

Key indicators of success were the students' perception of the program, the actions they took as a result of the program, and their academic record after the first semester. After the summer orientation program, students were sent a survey about the program as a whole and its specific components.

The survey responses, as a whole, were very positive. For example, 88 percent of the students reported that their overall experience was worthwhile. Ninety-three percent rated their interaction with the academic adviser as useful. Perhaps the most important consequence of the program, if we take the students' reports at face value, is that more than half of the students said they enrolled in different courses than they had initially considered as a result of the program. After the participants completed their first semester, their average GPA was calculated and compared to a parallel group of students who were also undeclared majors but who had not participated in the program. Students' grades at the end of the first semester clearly demonstrated that the program had had a positive effect in that those who participated in the program had a higher average GPA than their comparison group. They were also less likely to be on scholastic probation. Academic advising had influenced the choices students made and ultimately their academic success.

The information gathered about the students' academic performance and through this survey proved to be useful on many different levels: providing feedback to academic advisers, contributing to program changes, and keeping the administrators informed about students in general and the effectiveness of this academic advising. The results of this survey led to improvements in the program itself. Finally, an evaluative report was compiled and presented to administrators; this served to inform them and to reinforce their support for the program.

Summary

Next to limited parking and food in the residence hall that doesn't compare to home cooking, academic advising has been on the top ten list of student concerns for many years. Academic advising provides faculty members with an opportunity to influence the lives and careers of students. Like good teaching, effective advising requires the adviser to acquire a fund of knowledge and to be an effective communicator. The role of an adviser, however, is more interactive and personal than that of a classroom teacher. A good adviser helps students assess their academic goals, helps them plan their program of study, and keeps track of their academic progress. Most students will confront serious difficulties sometime during their college years, and it is at these turning points that the rapport a faculty member has established by taking the time to know the student pays off.

To help advisers establish closer, more useful, connections with students, colleges and universities need to work toward providing advisers with timely and genuinely useful information in an easily digestible form. Computer technology is now available to provide advisers with on-line data about the students they advise, but very few institutions of higher learning provide faculty advisers with such data. Until college- or university-wide advising systems are in place, most faculty advisers will have to continue to gather their own information from students, keep track of it, and bring it into discussions with students in a timely manner. Your efforts to get to know students—not just by being friendly with them—will create an atmosphere conducive to being an effective adviser.

GARY R. HANSON is coordinator for research in the Office of Admissions at the University of Texas at Austin. He does program evaluation and policy analysis for the Division of Student Affairs.

CHRISTINE HUSTON is coordinator for the Undergraduate Advising Center at the University of Texas at Austin. She oversees program development and evaluation as well as advises undergraduates.

This chapter considers various aspects of effective teaching and effective academic advising. Both occupations warrant professional status. In our analysis, it is concluded that effective academic advisers are teachers.

The Professional Status of Teachers and Academic Advisers: It Matters

Barbara K. Wade, Edgar P. Yoder

Several years ago, when speaking with a university department head, I heard a comment about a truck driver's statement on the national news. Discussing an impending national strike, the driver said, "Truck drivers are professionals and should be paid accordingly." We commented among other things, "So what is a professional? What occupations are professions?" The department head remarked, "I wonder if all full-time paid employees are professionals; I certainly don't think of truck driving as a profession." A nearby staff assistant immediately responded, "My brother is a truck driver and he is a professional!"

Arriving at the status of profession, especially within the academic community, is often perceived to be more difficult for the activities of both teaching and academic advising. Describing academic advising by itself as a profession is reminiscent of Smith's (1980) haunting characterization of teaching as a semi–profession. There are parallels between the activities of teaching and academic advising primarily when we attempt to describe tasks of teaching and advising as a profession rather than a semi-profession.

Teaching

The professional status of teachers has been a major theme in educational research throughout the nineteenth and twentieth centuries. To some extent, the ongoing struggle to professionalize teaching finds legitimacy in the field's affiliation with the science of psychology. Psychologists' construction of scientific theoretical knowledge bases about learning, development, motivation, personality, and intelligence subsequently impounds on the professionalization of teaching by virtue of its affiliation with psychology. Yet the idea of teaching being described as a semi-professional occupation persists.

According to Doyle (1990) the emergence of teaching as a profession depends on two beliefs: that the work of teaching is significant and that the public believes it is unable to conduct or evaluate this work on its own. Educational research describes how teachers make a difference. Doyle reports teaching effectiveness is measured in two areas: characteristics of teachers (personality, beliefs, attitudes, intelligence, preparation, and academic achievement) and behaviors of teachers (clarity, enthusiasm, warmth, frequency of praise, number of questions, etc.). Still, very serious issues surround attempts to predict success in teaching. Smith (1980) describes teaching as a semi-profession because of federal and state regulations imposed on the profession since the profession is unable or unwilling to set its own. Occupations such as lawyers, dentists, and physicians are considered professions, in part, because *the profession* has established entrance and licensing requirements and procedures, continuing education and professional development requirements, and a code of ethics governed by the membership.

Soder (1990) argues that similitude to other professions will not do because the "comparisons are inappropriate and self-defeating" (p. 76). He suggests establishing new criteria for defining a profession and recommends that four factors be considered in creating a new basis for the standards for professionalizing teaching: selection of individuals into programs; the nature of preservice training; processes for the selection of teachers; and the in-service continuing education and evaluation of teachers. Soder's four criteria do not address the situation in higher education, however. In higher education, faculty generally view themselves as members of a profession first (engineers, accountants, nurses, or mathematicians) and second as teachers in these fields.

Academic Advising

The teaching–learning process extends beyond the formal classroom setting. Theophitides, Terenzini, and Loring (1984) find that the extent of contact with faculty outside the formal classroom setting positively influences students' intellectual development.

Consequently, academic advising is directly related to retention. Students who are dissatisfied with academic advising do not persist within their schooling. Metzner (1989) reports that high-quality advising influences persistence with subsequent positive impact on grades and satisfaction. Beal and Noel (1980) report that college administrators rate inadequate advising as a major factor in student attrition. Other studies find similar types of results that relate persistence and success in college to the quality of academic advising, orientation programs, and freshman seminars (Upcraft and Gardner, 1989; Forrest, 1985; Pascarella and Terenzini, 1991). Yet academic advising is often not given the same status as instruction or research.

Academic advising also derives its legitimacy from the science of psychology in the areas of developmental theories and student change. Pascarella and Terenzini (1991) differentiate between change and developmental theories: "Change is qualitative and quantitative and implies no directionality whereas development suggests or implies a presumption of growth or the potential for growth" (p. 16). Academic advising influences traditional-aged college students at a time when remarkable growth and change are occurring as a result of the maturation process. To the extent that college students are emerging personalities with limited or no traditional community or family support systems immediately accessible, colleges and universities and academic advisers become central for support in numerous areas. O'Banion (1978) concludes that there are five essential areas for academic advising: exploration of life goals, exploration of vocational goals, choice of major area of study, course selection, and scheduling of courses.

Characteristics of effective advisers from administrators' and practitioners' perspectives (Metz, 1976) include being knowledgeable of university requirements, campus services, resources, programs, employment possibilities, campus programs, and how to "cut red tape." In addition, he reports, advisers need to take enough time to evaluate problems, be good listeners, show interest in students, be able to assess student capabilities, and get along with people. Students' perspectives include the need for advisers to be available, make an effort to know students as individuals, be knowledgeable about programs and requirements, be informed about graduation requirements, be caring people, be available to listen, know where students can go for additional information, and be capable of communicating to students that they enjoy and are committed to advising students.

Musser (1993) conducted a comprehensive literature review and interviewed administrators, academic advisers, faculty members, and students. This study by Musser identifies nine competencies necessary to be an effective academic adviser. The nine include communication, counseling, evaluation/assessment, interpersonal skills, knowledge base, management, philosophy/ethics of advising, positive attitude, and being a teacher.

The questions to be addressed are, When is academic advising effective teaching beyond just talk? What gaps exist between what was advised/taught and student outcomes? Finally, do academic advisers make a difference, and can academic advisers assess the impact of advising?

Teaching and Academic Advising

There exists a synergistic relationship between teaching and advising. The goals of teaching and academic advising are inherently the same since both reflect the goals of education. Cameron (1990), in summarizing the research of Stark and Lowther (1988), reports that personal growth of students is a goal of faculty across twelve disciplines. This personal growth has a common thread— the development of students' independent and critical thought processes. Illich

(1972) and Freire (1975) compellingly argue that the aims of education and educators are to help learners to do the following:

1. Understand themselves more fully and to maximize their potential
2. Develop a value system and understand the basis for their values
3. Develop critical analysis competence for solving problems
4. Understand the role of the individual within a local community and global society
5. Assume responsibility for their individual life-long learning

Teaching and advising both reflect an ongoing process requiring two-way communication between student and teacher or student and adviser. Effective teaching and effective advising reflect a developmental relationship that focuses on the needs and personal growth requirements of the student/advisee. Teaching is *not* telling, and advising is *not* telling. Telling or delivery of information for both the teacher and the adviser reflects a subprocess or activity in the learning or advising process. In fact, students do not appreciate teachers or advisers who do not effectively deliver the correct or appropriate information (Whaley, Heird, and Pritchett, 1994; Bedker and Young, 1994). Effective advising then requires a commitment; effective advising is not a perfunctory activity. It takes time and energy to guide the students' total development.

A subject area to consider when comparing teaching and advising is chemistry. A chemistry teacher imparts knowledge to students about the content of chemistry and may show the appearance and interactions of elements in a variety of ways in a laboratory. The chemistry teacher guides students through experiments and perhaps demonstrates the disagreeable consequences of inappropriately mixing elements. The teacher may show, tell, or assist students in discovering new information.

An academic adviser may assist the student in knowing the many programs available within the institution and may guide the student to explore various majors and eventually declare one. The academic adviser might help the student discover strengths and weaknesses that relate to choosing a particular major. For example, the risk for a student inadequately prepared in science entering an engineering field has very specific consequences; he or she will need to take additional credits to graduate. The academic adviser might assist a student in exploring appropriate mixes between the student's interests and abilities. The academic adviser teaches the student in an informal setting about choices and procedures for successfully completing a specific degree.

Effective teachers and effective academic advisers share characteristics and behaviors. Both effective teachers and academic advisers are caring, good listeners, knowledgeable about their content areas, and prepared. Both believe in the human dignity of all their students. Their behaviors reflect clarity, enthusiasm, warmth, flexibility, availability, and businesslike, task-oriented behaviors. Equally important are students' opportunities to obtain information provided by the teacher or the academic adviser.

We contend that teaching and advising are aspects of educational mentoring that are essential to developing the educated undergraduate student. This mentoring occurs in the formal classroom setting and in our day-to-day interaction with students outside the classroom. In essence, we teach and advise in our day-to-day interaction with our students and advisees. As advisers, we teach as much through our advising efforts as we do via the delivery of a formal lecture.

Who Cares?

To be or not to be a professional—does anybody care? Soder (1990) suggests that the definition of "professional" emerges from the perceptions of the individuals claiming to be professionals and those who accept those claims. Teachers and academic advisers, while claiming to be professionals, struggle to persuade others to accept their claims. These claims influence policy, practice, and rewards associated with the status and security of being a professional.

To be regarded as a professional is the collective responsibility of those who advise as we continue to define and describe the rights, roles, and the responsibilities of academic advisers while establishing standards and practices for the activity. The goals of quality teaching, advising, and research must remain central to the goals of higher education. When enrollment declines, institutions of higher education grow more financially dependent on tuition revenues. Quality academic advising and teaching are essential components for retaining students. To professionalize teaching and academic advising underscores their significance and value.

References

Beal, P. and Noel, L. (1980). *What Works in Student Retention?* Iowa City, Iowa: American College Testing Program and the National Center for Higher Education Management Systems, 1980. (ED 197 635).

Bedker, P.D. and Young, A. J. "Advising in the 90s: Assessing the Quality of the Advisor/Advisee Relationship." *NACTA Journal*, 1994, *38,* 33–36.

Cameron, B. "Personal Growth as a Faculty Goal for Students." In Joscelyn, M. K. (ed.), *Accent on Improving College Teaching and Learning*, no 10. Ann Arbor: The National Center for the Improvement of Teaching and Learning, The University of Michigan, 1990.

Doyle, W. "Themes in Teacher Education Research." In Houston, W. R. (ed.), *Handbook of Research on Teacher Education*. New York: Macmillan, 1990.

Forrest, A. "Creating Conditions for Student and Institutional Success." In Levitz, L., Levitz, D., and Saluri, D. (eds.), *Increasing Student Retention: Effective Programs and Practices for Reducing the Dropout Rate*. San Francisco: Jossey-Bass, 1985.

Freire, P. *Pedagogy of the Oppressed*. New York: The Seabury Press, 1975.

Illich, I. *Deschooling Society*. New York: Harper and Row, 1972.

Metz, J. *Academic Advisement: Personnel and Preparation*. (ERIC Document Reproduction Service No. ED 133 631), 1976.

Metzner, B. "Perceived Quality of Academic Advising: The Effect on Freshman Attrition." *American Educational Research Journal*, 1989, *16*(1), 422–442.

Musser, T. "Perceptions of Professional Advisors, Faculty, Administrators and Students of the Competencies Needed to Be an Effective Academic Adviser." Unpublished Master's Thesis. University Park: The Pennsylvania State University, 1993.

O'Banion, T. "Skills, Knowledge, and Attitudes Required for Good Academic Advising." In Crockett, D. S., (ed.), *Academic Advising: A Resource Document.* Iowa City: The American College Testing Program, 1978.

Pascarella, E. T., and Terenzini, P. D. *How College Affects Students: Findings from Twenty Years of Research.* San Francisco: Jossey-Bass, 1991.

Smith, B. O. *A Design for School Pedagogy.* Washington, D.C.: U.S. Department of Education, 1980.

Soder, R. "The Rhetoric of Teacher Professionalization." In Goodlad, J. I., Soder, R., and Sirotnik, K. A. (eds.), *Moral Dimensions of Teaching.* San Francisco: Jossey-Bass, 1990.

Stark, J. S. and Lowther, M. A. *Strengthening the Ties That Bind: Integrating Undergraduate Liberal and Professional Study.* Ann Arbor: The University of Michigan, 1988.

Theophitides, C., Terenzini P., and Loring, W. (1984). "The Relationship Between Freshman Year Experience and Perceived Importance of Four Major Educational Goals." *Research in Higher Education,* 1984, 20(2), 235–252.

Upcraft, L., and Gardner, J. (1989). *The Freshman Year Experience: Helping Students Survive and Succeed in College.* San Francisco: Jossey-Bass 1989.

Whaley, D., Heird, J. C., and Pritchett, J. "Taking the Pulse: A Case Study of Undergraduate Agriculture Students' Opinions." *NACTA Journal,* 1994, 38(1), 37–41.

BARBARA K. WADE *is senior programs coordinator, Division of Undergraduate Studies, College of Agricultural Sciences, The Pennsylvania State University, University Park.*

EDGAR P. YODER *is professor of agricultural and extension education, College of Agricultural Sciences, The Pennsylvania State University, University Park.*

*This chapter introduces the many resources available to faculty
advisers who are interested in improving the advising services on their
campus, are interested in learning more about the field of academic
advising, or wish to perform research in this area.*

Resources for Academic Advising

Virginia N. Gordon

The number of resources pertaining to academic advising at the national level
has expanded dramatically in the past two decades. Many advisers, especially
faculty advisers from different disciplines, often are not aware of the vast array
of resources pertaining specifically to academic advising. This chapter will out-
line many of the resources now available to advisers, administrators, and students who have a direct or peripheral interest in this topic. The resources
described below are not all inclusive of those available to the faculty adviser,
but they represent some of the most readily available and useful ones.

Publications

Publications about academic advising fall into two categories: (1) those written specifically on the subject (for example, advising delivery systems, professional advisers), and (2) those written on topics that indirectly relate to
advising (for example, legal issues in higher education, counseling learning
disabled students). The publications described below include books, journals,
annotated bibliographies, and other related printed material.

Books

The following books relate directly to the topic of academic advising. The
annotations illustrate how academic advising can be viewed from many different perspectives.

Frost, S. H. *Academic Advising for Student Success: A System of Shared Responsibility.* ASHE-ERIC Higher Education Report No. 3. Washington, D.C.: The
George Washington University, 1991.

NEW DIRECTIONS FOR TEACHING AND LEARNING, no. 62, Summer 1995 © Jossey-Bass Publishers

This report focuses on "outcomes of advising in the context of research on contact between faculty and students, students' involvement, and persistence." The information in this book is appropriate for those working to increase the positive outcomes of college through academic advising.

Gordon, V. N. *Academic Advising: An Annotated Bibliography.* Westport, Conn: Greenwood Press, 1994.

This collection of annotated bibliographies represents an overview of the many and varied topics associated with academic advising. Included are 351 citations contained within ten topical areas (for example, organizational and delivery systems, developmental advising, special populations, culturally diverse students, adviser training, advising as a profession, career advising).

Gordon, V. N. *Handbook of Academic advising.* Westport, Conn: Greenwood Press, 1992.

This book is intended to assist practitioners in the intricacies of advising students. It describes different organizational models for delivering services, outlines the basic tasks involved in the advising process, and summarizes advising approaches for the many special and diverse student populations that advisers encounter. The vast wellspring of literature applying to academic advising from many disciplines is the foundation supporting the information imparted in this book.

Grites, T. J. *Academic Advising: Getting Us Through the Eighties.* AAHE-ERIC Higher Education Research Report No. 7. Washington, D.C.: The George Washington University, 1979.

This research report takes a comprehensive look at the academic advising process. Historical developments, delivery systems, and interinstitutional interfacing of academic advising are reviewed. Eight recommendations for assessing advising programs are offered.

Habley, W. R. (ed.). *The Status and Future of Academic Advising—Problems and Promises.* Iowa City: The American College Testing Program (ACT) National Center for the Advancement of Educational Practices, 1988.

This volume provides an in-depth look at topics consistently viewed as critical to the success of advising programs. In addition to a summary of the Third ACT National Survey of Academic Advising, there are chapters on such topics as organizing advising services, developmental advising, adviser training, and evaluation. Exemplary advising programs are also described.

King, M. C. (ed.). *Academic Advising: Organizing and Delivery Services for Student Success.* New Directions for Community Colleges, No. 82. San Francisco: Jossey-Bass, 1993.

This volume views academic advising as the only structured service on college campuses that guarantees students' interaction with concerned representatives of the institution. It defines developmental advising, describes the ways in which advising services are organized and delivered, and discusses the key components of effective advising programs. Although geared to community colleges, much of the information is relevant to other types of institutions.

Schein, H. K., Laff, N.S., and Allen, D. R. *Giving Advice to Students: A Road Map for College Professionals.* Alexandria, Va: American College Personnel Association, 1987.

This monograph uses student needs as the basis for cooperation between academic and student affairs. Root concepts and critical thinking skills that underlie all learning are incorporated into a developmental advising scheme. Five central elements of academic advising are discussed: academic decision making, resource identification and use, career search, postgraduate studies, and counseling.

Winston, R. B., Jr., Ender, S. C., and Miller, T. K. (eds.). *Developmental Approaches to Academic Advising.* New Directions for Student Services, No. 17. San Francisco: Jossey-Bass, 1982.

Student development concepts are the focus for detailing useful advising practices. The academic advising process presents an opportunity for incorporating student development concepts beyond the realm of traditional programming. An integrated approach to educating students that addresses personal as well as intellectual development throughout the institution is espoused.

Winston, R. B., Jr., Miller, T. K., Ender, S. C., and Grites, T. J. (eds.) *Developmental Academic Advising.* San Francisco: Jossey-Bass, 1984.

This book provides a comprehensive examination of academic advising from a developmental perspective. The seventeen chapters show how advising programs can enhance the quality of students' educational experiences, help them adjust to the college environment, and help them achieve educational, personal, and career goals. Responsible advising programs can also further an institution's mission and goals and decrease attrition resulting from a lack of effective advising and mentoring.

Professional Journals

The journal of the National Academic Advising Association (NACADA) focuses specifically on academic advising, but other journals contain articles about advising as well as on related topics. Many of these journal articles discuss the research and practice of advising by faculty members. The following list offers a sampling of the scope of professional journals that contain articles pertaining to academic advising.

NACADA Journal
Journal of College Student Development
NASPA Journal
Community College Journal of Research and Practice
College and University
Research in Higher Education
Journal of the Freshman Year Experience
Journal of Counseling and Development
Career Development Quarterly

Professional journals that are discipline-oriented, such as the *Teaching of Psychology, Journal of Medical Education, Engineering Education* and *Journalism Educator,* also contain articles about academic advising.

Annotated Bibliographies

In addition to the book *Academic Advising: An Annotated Bibliography*, the most widely used resource for annotated bibliographies on the topic of academic advising is the *National Clearinghouse for Academic Advising* at the Ohio State University. Orders may be placed for paper copies or 3.5-inch computer diskettes in WordPerfect 5.1. (This service is free to NACADA members; a small charge is assessed to nonmembers to cover the cost of reproducing and postage.) The following is a partial list of over fifty-five topics for which bibliographies are available from the National Clearinghouse for Academic Advising, University College, 110 Enarson Hall, the Ohio State University, Columbus, Ohio 43210.

Adviser Training
Legal Issues
Students in Academic Difficulty
Student Retention
Educational Aspirations of College Students
Faculty Advising
Evaluation and Assessment
Career Advising and Decision Making
Undecided Student Advising
Sexual Harassment
Freshman Advising
Mentoring
Ethical Concerns in Advising

The director of the Clearinghouse also annotates the most recent journals and other offerings on advising in a section in each issue of the *NACADA Journal*. The ERIC (Educational Resource Information Center) data base is another well-known source of citations from the current literature and includes academic advising and related subjects. Most ERIC resources may be read on microfiche or obtained in paper form from EDRS (Educational Document Reproduction Service). College librarians will be able to direct you to these documents. Paper copies may be obtained for a fee by calling 1-800-443-ERIC. A few examples follow:

Kramer, H. C., and Gardener, R. E. *Advising by Faculty* (rev. ed.). Washington, D.C.: National Education Association. (ERIC Document Reproduction Service No. Ed 235 742), 1983.

McMillian, M., and K. McKinney. *Strategies for Effective Undergraduate Advising in Sociology.* Resource material for teaching. Washington, D.C.: American Sociological Association, Teaching Resource Center. (ERIC Document Reproduction Service No. ED 273 209), 1985.

Benson, M. T. (ed). *A Statistical Analysis of the Predictions of Graduation Rates for College Student Athletes.* NCAA Academic Performance Study (Report 91-02). Overland Park, Kan.: National Collegiate Athletic Association. (ERIC Document Reproduction Service No. ED 335 991), 1991.

Other Publications

The American College Testing Program (ACT) has published many reports and monographs relating to academic advising:

Fulfilling the Promise?

This is the final report of the ACT Fourth National Survey of Academic Advising (1993). The surveys have provided a baseline for practitioners "to assess the quality of advising on their own campuses."

Academic Advising Audit.

The audit is designed to help institutions evaluate and analyze the organization an delivery of advising services on their campus (1993). Results of the audit should reveal "areas of strength and areas where improvement may be needed."

Advising Skills, Techniques, and Resources.

This resource document contains articles and materials from many different types of institutions designed to enhance all phases of academic advising (1989). Topics include an introduction to advising, training, skills, techniques, and resources, evaluation, and ACT materials used for advising.

Pathways to Persistence.

This is a role-play simulation exercise for use in adviser training based on Tinto's model (1988).

The Status and Future of Academic Advising.

Described earlier, this resource can be obtained from the NACADA National Office. Information about the other publications can be obtained from the American College Testing Program.

NACADA Newsletter.

The "Academic Advising News" is published four times a year and focuses on Association news, information about members, and key issues in advising. The newsletter is sent to every NACADA member.

NACADA Reports and Monographs.

Task Force Reports, National Conference Proceedings, and monographs are available from the NACADA Executive Office. A report, "Designing an Effective Adviser Training Program," is available on a 3.5-inch diskette.

National Organizations and Conferences

National Academic Advising Association (NACADA).

The purpose of NACADA is "to promote the quality of academic advising in institutions of higher education, and as an organization of professional advisers, faculty, and students of such institutions, to ensure the educational development of students." NACADA's constituency consists of faculty members, administrators, counselors and others in academic and student affairs.

In addition to the *NACADA Journal, Newsletter* and other publications described above, NACADA sponsors one national and ten regional meetings each year. The Summer Institute on Academic Advising is co-sponsored by NACADA and the American College Testing Program (ACT) in June or July and provides an in-depth study of academic advising.

NACADA also sponsors many awards and scholarships, including the Pacesetter Award that recognizes chief executive officers, provosts, and chief academic or student affairs officers who exemplify a commitment to advising and are true advocates for students and advisers. A graduate education scholarship is awarded to a NACADA member who is currently enrolled in either a master's or doctoral program. A research support program provides grants of up to $5,000 for individual research that contributes to the field of advising-related research. Faculty, professional advisers, and graduate students are eligible for this support.

The National Recognition Program for Academic Advising is sponsored by NACADA and the American College Testing Program (ACT). The purpose of the program is to recognize individual advisers who have demonstrated the qualities associated with outstanding academic advising of students. Outstanding Institutional Advising Program awards are also given through this program.

NACADA also sponsors a Consultants Bureau to provide assistance to and promote quality academic advising practices in colleges and universities. Examples of consulting services include advising program review, computer-assisted advising, evaluation of advising, training advisers, and speakers on advising topics.

A Placement Service is sponsored by NACADA to facilitate the job search activities of members of the Association by listing both employers and applicants. Both may review listings and contact one another through this service.

NACADA Commissions address a broad spectrum of interests and concerns including adult learners, advising administration, graduate student advising, multicultural concerns, and standards and ethics.

National Association of Academic Affairs Administrators (AcAfAd).

This organization serves the "interests and needs of persons responsible for the development, administration, and implementation of academic policies, programs and services at institutions of higher education." AcAfAd is an affiliate of the American College Personnel Association (ACPA). Academic advisement administrators are included as members. There are five regional alignments that hold meetings annually. Management development seminars are held annually to help new "middle management administrators to share in the knowledge and expertise of their colleagues and peers." *AcAfAd* gives one national and two regional awards to recognize members' contributions to the association. *AcAfAd Newsletter* is published three times a year.

Local Advising Organizations

Advisers in some institutions (particularly large universities) have formed advising organizations or groups to bring together professional advisers, student affairs administrators, and faculty on a regular basis. These groups may or may not be affiliated with NACADA. The purpose of these organizations is to advance the cause of academic advising on that particular campus and to promote adviser development and training.

National Clearinghouse for Academic Advising

In addition to the annotated bibliographies mentioned above, the *National Clearinghouse for Academic Advising* serves as a repository for other information pertaining to academic advising. Examples of adviser handbooks, institutional advising, mission statements, training manuals, computer programs, and other advising materials are available. The Clearinghouse not only disseminates information, but also seeks advising related materials from many sources for deposit and eventual sharing.

Advising Standards

The *Council for the Advancement of Standards in Higher Education (CAS)* was established in 1979 and represents an ever-growing consortium of higher education professional associations. CAS was created to "establish, disseminate, and advocate professional standards and guidelines on a nationwide basis for higher education programs and services." The standards for academic advising are set in program, organization and administration, human resources, funding, facilities, campus and community relations, ethics, and evaluation. Standards and guidelines are also provided for the purpose or mission of advising.

Directory of Resources

The following is a list of organizations and their addresses described in this chapter.

American College Testing Program (ACT), 2201 N. Dodge Street, P.O. Box 168, Iowa City, Iowa 52243, (319) 337-1035.

Council for the Advancement of Standards in Higher Education, 2108 Mitchell Building, University of Maryland at College Park College Park, Md. 20742-5521, (301) 314-8478.

ERIC Document Reproduction Service (EDRS), 7420 Fullerton Road Suite 110, Springfield, Va. 22153, 1-800-443-ERIC

National Academic Advising Association (NACADA), Kansas State University, 2323 Anderson Avenue, Manhattan, Kan. 66502, (913) 532-5717.

National Association of Academic Affairs Administrators (AcAfAd), Gillum Hall, 201F, Indiana State University, Terre Haute, Ind. 47809, (812) 237-2700.

National Clearinghouse for Academic Advising, The Ohio State University, 110 Enarson Hall, 154 W. 12th Avenue, Columbus, OH 43210, (614) 292-6344.

Summary

This chapter has introduced the many resources available to faculty advisers who are interested in improving the advising services on their campus, are interested in learning more about the field of academic advising, or are interested in performing research in this area.

Crookston (1972) suggested that advising must be concerned with "facilitating the student's rational processes, environmental and interpersonal interactions, behavioral awareness, problem-solving, decision-making and evaluation skills." He insisted that these are not only advising functions, but teaching functions as well. In the dual role of faculty adviser and teacher, embracing the perspective that "advising is teaching" can have a profound effect on the relationships between advisers and advisees. By becoming more involved with some of the resources described in this chapter, faculty advisers can not only broaden their own knowledge and skills, but can also enrich their contacts with students through a deeper understanding of how important this function can become in that relationship.

Reference

Crookston, B. B. "Developmental View of Academic Advising as Teaching." *Journal of College Student Personnel,* 1972, *13,* 12–16.

VIRGINIA N. GORDON teaches graduate and undergraduate level courses in the College of Education at the Ohio State University and is assistant dean emeritus of University College. She is the author of numerous books and journal articles and is past president of the National Academic Advising Association.

INDEX

Academic adviser(s). *See also* Faculty adviser(s): advice to, 75–76; availability of, 18; as helper, educator, and mentor, 14–15; incentives for, 18–20, 65; as professional, 97–101; Academic advising, 1–3, 72–73; in arts, 43–54;assessment, 87–96; benefits of, 8–9; co-curricular activities and, 39; complexity of, 16; computer-based systems for, 70; data collection regarding, 56–57; definition of, 22–23; effectiveness of, 94–96; faculty attitudes about, 13–24; flexibility of, 9; future trends in, 69–70; importance of, 20–22, 56, 95; instructional requirements and, 38–39; negative aspects of, 15; organizations and conferences promoting, 108–110; process of, 92–94; resources for, 39–40, 103–110; responsibility for, 6–7, 22; in science and engineering, 65–70; in social sciences, 55–62; of special student populations, 28–33; :teaching and, 36, 99–101; :training needed in, 16–20 use of, 89–90; women in nontraditional fields, 71–76
*Academic Advising: An Annotated Bibliography,*106
AcAfAd. *See* National Association of Academic Affairs Administrators (AcAfAd)
ACPA. *See* American College Personnel Association (ACPA)
ACT. *See* American College Testing Program (ACT)
Administrator(s)
need for education in advising, 16–20; view on academic advising, 5–10
Allen, D. R., 105
American College Personnel Association (ACPA), 109
American College Testing Program (ACT), 35, 107–108, 110
American Economic Association, 62
American Political Science Association, 62
American Psychological Association, 62
American Sociological Association, 62
Americans with Disabilities Act of 1990, 31
Anderson, E., 80, 85

Arts advising, 43–54; art as work, 48; in changing world, 52–53; experience as teacher, 48–49; failure and, 46; honesty in, 44–45; individualism and, 49–51; supply and demand concerns in, 46; survival of arts and, 53–54; talent and, 46;
Assessment, 88–89; academic advising and, 87–96; data, 91–92
definition of, 88
Association of American Colleges, 26, 34
Astin, A. W., 26, 34

Beal, P., 98, 101
Bedker, P. D., 100–101
Benson, M. T., 107
Berdahl, R. M., 5–11
Betz, N. E., 76–77
Boyer, E. L., 6, 10

Cameron, B., 99, 101
Campbell, J., 23–24
Career Development Quarterly, 106
Career information, 39
CAS. *See* Council for the Advancement of Standards in Higher Education (CAS)
Chickering, A., 37, 41
The Chronicle of Higher Education, 31, 34
Cogdell, J. R., 65–70
Cohen, J., 31, 34
College and University, 106
Community College Journal of Research and Practice, 106
Computer-based advising, 70
Conwell, E. M., 73, 77
Council for Advancement of Standards in Higher Education, 110
Council for the Advancement of Standards in Higher Education (CAS), 110
Crookston, B. B., 110
Curriculum requirements, 38

Discover, 30
Dorfman, J., 57, 62
Doyle, W., 98, 102
Dresselhaus, M. S., 73, 77

ORDERING INFORMATION

NEW DIRECTIONS FOR TEACHING AND LEARNING is a series of paperback books that presents ideas and techniques for improving college teaching, based both on the practical expertise of seasoned instructors and on the latest research findings of educational and psychological researchers. Books in the series are published quarterly in spring, summer, fall, and winter and are available for purchase by subscription as well as by single copy.

SUBSCRIPTIONS for 1995 cost $48.00 for individuals (a savings of 25 percent over single-copy prices) and $64.00 for institutions, agencies, and libraries. Please do not send institutional checks for personal subscriptions. Standing orders are accepted.

SINGLE COPIES cost $16.95 plus shipping (see below) when payment accompanies order. California, New Jersey, New York, and Washington, D.C., residents please include appropriate sales tax. Canadian residents add GST and any local taxes. Billed orders will be charged shipping and handling. No billed shipments to post office boxes. Orders from outside the United States or Canada *must be prepaid* in U.S. dollars or charged to VISA, MasterCard, or American Express.

SHIPPING (SINGLE COPIES ONLY): one issue, add $3.50; two issues, add $4.50; three to four issues, add $5.50; five issues, add $6.50; six to eight issues, add $7.50; nine or more issues, add $8.50.

DISCOUNTS FOR QUANTITY ORDERS are available. Please write to the address below for information.

ALL ORDERS must include either the name of an individual or an official purchase order number. Please submit your order as follows:
    Subscriptions: specify series and year subscription is to begin
    Single copies: include individual title code (such as TL54)

MAIL ALL ORDERS TO:
    Jossey-Bass Publishers
    350 Sansome Street
    San Francisco, CA 94104-1342

FOR SUBSCRIPTION SALES OUTSIDE OF THE UNITED STATES, CONTACT:
    any international subscription agency or Jossey-Bass directly.

OTHER TITLES AVAILABLE IN THE
NEW DIRECTIONS FOR TEACHING AND LEARNING SERIES
Robert J. Menges, Editor-in-Chief
Marilla D. Svinicki, Associate Editor